Donald Barthelme

Donald Barthelme

AN EXHIBITION

Jerome Klinkowitz

Duke University Press

Durham & London 1991

for Ihab Hassan

Contents

Acknowledgments and

a Note on the Texts

D onald Barthelme: An Exhibition was begun as a lively, contemporaneous affair in May 1989, as part of my preparation for a lecture to Professor Ihab Hassan's seminar on postmodernism at the University of Wisconsin–Milwaukee's Center for Twentieth Century Studies. The lecture and subsequent discussions took place on July 20, after which I returned home for more work on the book. At which point Richard Kostelanetz phoned from New York with the news of my subject's death.

As will be apparent from my approach to his works, which has taken the form of a retrospective exhibition meant to highlight the centrality of The Dead Father to his canon, Donald Barthelme was exceptionally generous, letting me poke in and around his personal and professional life far beyond the conventions of customary interviews. In another context, his and my friend Kurt Vonnegut described this style of scholarship as "therapeutic vivisection," something most contemporary authors have to suffer now and then. Don's patience with these probings and slicings, however, was nothing short of remarkable. In heaven there is no beer—nor J. & B. scotch, fax machines, phones, or even mail deliveries. We have God to thank for that, and Donald Barthelme to thank for sharing so much information while he was alive.

In the long haul of working on Barthelme's writing I must thank Asa Pieratt and Robert Murray Davis for collaborating with me on the first Barthelme bibliography in 1977 and Julie Huffman-klinkowitz for keeping it updated since. I'm grateful to Ihab Hassan for getting me interested in The Dead Father as a central text, and to the University of Northern Iowa for believing in my work; once again, the university has been my sole source of support for this project, in this case a direct grant from the office of President Constantine W. Curris followed by a Summer Research Fellowship from our Graduate College.

All quotations are taken from the first editions of Donald Barthelme's novels, essays, and short story collections (which are referred to by page reference and abbreviated title as keyed in my concluding bibliography), or from individual magazines and books edited by others in cases where the material had not yet been collected by Barthelme (with full citations in the bibliography). Special thanks are due to *The New Yorker* for identifying unsigned contributions to the "Comment" section of the magazine's "Talk of the Town" pages.

Donald Barthelme

Prologue:

With Don in the Village

It was a leafy and still bright early evening, in the mid-October season that makes New York City a most attractively livable place. For years, when writing Don Barthelme at his West Eleventh Street address, I'd pictured it like the other areas of Greenwich Village known from previous trips: the bustling street life around Washington Square, the lofts along Crosby and Spring streets, or even the broad openness and commercial desolation I'd seen down Hudson Street. That's where I'd found Clarence Major, Steve Katz, Michael Stephens, and Gil Sorrentino, and their apartments had each seemed in turn the ideal place from which to launch a literary revolution. But West Eleventh was something surprisingly new. No tall buildings—just a row on each side of semi-detached town houses and flats two or at the most three stories high, with front steps leading down into well-kept, neatly fenced little front yards. One could barely hear the traffic swishing along Sixth Avenue to the east, and after a few steps from the Seventh Avenue subway its urban rumble faded away, replaced by birdsong in the trees and the soft conversation of residents out walking their dogs, heading off to dinner, or lounging on their front steps as casual and secure as any Midwestern small town dwellers.

It was a side of New York I'd never seen, and hadn't associated with Donald Barthelme. Yet it was part of his textual identity, albeit unsigned—he'd been writing informal pieces within the anonymity of the "Comment" section from The New Yorker's introductory "Talk of the Town" pages for years, and just about this time the ambience of life in and around West Eleventh Street had begun taking a prominent part in these ruminations and descriptions. My bibliography work would reveal their authorship, and Barthelme himself seemed sufficiently pleased with their quality to collect them a few years later in a small press edition, *Here in the Village*. But on this early October evening of 1975, that side of him was something I'd yet to uncover and appreciate.

Finding his address near mid-block, I opened the yard's wrought iron gate and headed toward the stairs. Inside the vestibule were several mailboxes and doorbells, one of which bore a punched plastic label reading "Barthelme/Knox." But below it was another message, a torn scrap of typewritten bond paper advising "doorbell broken, stand at window and yell."

I'd noticed the tall window overlooking the yard, and so hurried back down the stairs to do as bidden. And now the pleasant environs of this quiet, shady street became a stage for some Barthelme-scripted histrionics, as I positioned myself beneath the glass and called out, "Don! Oh Don! Hey, Don!"

Barthelme's text, of course, had turned me into a character in his fiction, a thirty-one-year-old professor and literary critic made to feel like a little kid calling from the front yard for his friend. It was the tactic of "Me and Miss Mandible," Barthelme's first published story, dating back to 1961 and stamping *Come Back, Dr. Caligari* as a collection uncommonly taken with social signs and their deliberative use in contemporary life. In that piece the narrator finds himself, as a grown man, thrust back into a sixth-grade classroom, where he must suffer the growing pains and tribulations of pubescent youth from the awkward position of superior knowledge and experience. The character feels ridiculous, of course, as I did out underneath Don's window. Whether intended or not, the exercise put me at the author's advantage; I was firmly inside his text.

Working my way out of that transcription became the evening's challenge, and in Barthelme's new wife—Marion Knox—I found a helpful ally. A dozen or so years younger than Don, she was about my age, and firmly on my side of the generation gap that being born in 1943 as opposed to 1931 can create. After introductions, a scotch on ice, and small talk we walked down to Hopper's on Sixth Avenue, a recently opened but already trendy Village restaurant. Another drink or two put Barthelme in fine social fettle, and to my and Marion's discomfort he began a bit of fictive play with the waiter. The young man had no sooner given his pro forma introduction—

"Good evening, my name is William. I'll be your waiter . . . have you seen the menu?"—when Don interrupted him with a sharpness that startled us all.

"No you're not!" Barthelme snapped, his try at mock stuffiness coming off much harsher than he'd meant.

"Sir?" the waiter stuttered, as taken aback as Marion and I.

"You are not a waiter," Don insisted, and began weaving a necessary fiction for the young man. "You're an actor, or a musician. Or a painter. A sculptor perhaps? But not really a waiter! This is Greenwich Village, after all. You're a struggling artist, waiting tables while waiting for a break. So please don't say you're a waiter!"

Rustling his napkin, Don drew himself toward the table as if the matter were settled. But it wasn't, for William was not about to be caught for the next hour within Barthelme's text.

"I'm sorry, sir," he stated with the firmness Don had sought for but misplayed at the start. "I am a waiter, and a damn good one. May I please have your order?"

With William now generating the narrative, Don sulkily dropped out. I ordered lamb, Marion chose the same, and ordered a chicken Kiev for her husband, who kept silent until the waiter had left. Only after the meal had been served and eaten did Barthelme resume the little narrative begun so badly long before. "I tell you, the young man really is an actor or some such," he murmured quite audibly to me as William reached for the check. But now Don felt in control, for lying atop the bill was his American Express credit card, its raised letters shouting out the legend "Donald Barthelme" for poor William to take in. Forgotten was the arrangement that I was treating Don and Marion to dinner, so important was it for the author to sign his story.

Back at Barthelme's apartment, the evening was filled with literary talk and scotches. As the hour drew toward midnight, Don reached behind him for a copy of my Literary Disruptions and ran down its table of contents, checking off who belonged in this study of the decade's innovators and who didn't. "Now if you want to be the top dog critic," he advised, "you're going to have to be right more often than you're wrong." His appraisal of my book was generous, but gave my choices only the slightest winning edge. "Five out of eight isn't bad," I said. "That's hitting .625, an amazing stat for any league." "No it isn't," Don replied abruptly, with the same awkwardly feigned sharpness he'd blundered in the restaurant. "I'm the hitter. You're the fielder. And you're going to have to stop dropping three balls for every five you catch!"

At this point Marion came to my rescue. Don's occasional shows of pomp and bluster had driven her away earlier, to take refuge in her study down the hall. Now she had returned, standing behind Don's chair where he could hear but not see her. And what she had to say was startling indeed.

"Why Donald!" she announced in a tone of mock dismay. Smiling at what wonder of his she was about to admire, he reached for his drink and took a long satisfied sip as she continued: "Your father's is bigger than yours!"

With a hideous choke Don spit out his scotch and leaned forward, gasping for breath. In a moment he was OK, and Marion met my worried glance with a broad smile. In her hand was the latest edition of *Who's Who in America*, opened apparently to the page where Donald Barthelme, Junior and Senior, were biographically profiled. Turning around, her flushed and shaking husband could now see that. But for her little trick and the awareness it prompted he didn't have a word.

And so the ultimate text, on which he'd been laboring for all his life with his life, had done him in—by being less than his father's. The narrative could not have been better or more revealing, even if drawn out by Sigmund Freud or analyzed by Jacques Lacan. Completing this textually generated story was something I'd saved for the night's end—an advance copy of Don's new novel which I'd pried loose from a friend at the Strand Book Store just hours before. It was, of course, *The Dead Father*, and getting Don's inscription turned out to be the most appropriate coda imaginable to this fiction-filled evening.

Marion's little trick, of course, was more than just a deflatingly satirical comment on her husband's behavior that night. It was funny according to the terms of the awkward games he'd been playing, but its brilliance derived from its ability to seize upon so many themes and attitudes Don himself had been exploiting in his work. The rivalry (and inevitable perception of inferiority) with his father was a natural link between Marion's joke and his new novel, and the book itself seemed a natural consequence of his previous work and the critical reaction to it. If the novel can be considered the "big daddy" of fictive forms—Hemingway's heavy-weight that can go the distance, James's loose, baggy monster that overruns all limits of constraint—then Donald Barthelme's most successful form, the short story, would have to be considered junior in comparison. Moreover, his stories themselves always threatened to break down into even smaller units. Lines of dialogue could hang there as if disembodied from the narrative, short paragraphs might stand in apposition rather than in any conventional sense of development, and the narrative itself would cohere less in terms of logical sequence than as an appealingly offbeat assemblage of fragments. "Fragments are the only forms I trust," says a character in one of Barthelme's earlier stories, "See the Moon?" Because of the critical environment of these same mid-1960s, when Barthelme's first collections appeared, this motto became a younger generation of fiction writers' sassy response to the lofty dictum that the novel was dead, outdated by a cultural style and pace beyond the scope of its essentially nineteenth-century conventions. Yet could the most imitated fictionist of this generation transform his mastery of short fiction fragments into a new form of novel? The Dead Father was Barthelme's specific response to this challenge.

With Donald Barthelme's canon of works now complete, it is possible to see how central is this novel to his accomplishments as a fiction writer. Historically, it stands at the center of his career, coming fourteen years after his first serious work and fourteen years before 1989, when his last short story to be published in his lifetime would appear, as had most of his work, in The New Yorker. The same three-decade structure locates it almost equidistantly between his other two novels, Snow White (1967) and Paradise (1986). Stylistically, The Dead Father signals key developments in Barthelme's art that one can anticipate in the works that precede it and that prove themselves obvious in his fiction of the later 1970s and 1980s. Thematically, the author's particular interests and fancies—so deftly exploited by Marion's sly joke that evening in 1975—are even more apparent in their development among these three novels, with The Dead Father serving as the fulcrum that turns playful satire into more considered analysis. In terms of its topic, Snow White is a novel of sons—dwarfish and inconsequential sons to be sure, as they work and play in the liberated context of a Greenwich Village apartment graced by the presence of a shared paramour, the lovely Grimm brothers and Disney heroine whom their failures make more of a mother substitute than mate. *Paradise*, on the other hand, gives readers a single grown man—once a son, now a putative father—whose world is taken over by the discourses of three young women who move into that same Village apartment, a residence Barthelme himself had assumed in the early 1960s after leaving home in Houston. Only in *The Dead Father* itself do we see the key structural terms—not just sons and women involved with them, but the son's father caught in transition among the competing forces of his own decline, a son's ascendancy, and the women's increasing desire for a say in matters.

Looking forward and back, one sees that *The Dead Father* employs the broad range of Barthelme's strongest talents both as a short fiction writer and as a novelist. Like so many of his contemporaries, including Kurt Vonnegut and Richard Brautigan, he writes a short novel composed of many chapters (twenty-three for just 175 pages of text). Like Raymond Federman, Ronald Sukenick, and Steve Katz, he places a work inside the work, in this case the self-containable "Manual for Sons," which appeared as a short story in *The New Yorker* and boasts no less than twenty-three sub-chapters itself. But overall the strongest affinity Barthelme shows is with himself, with the highly distinguishable features of his literary talent that for the past decade had made his stories so immediately recognizable, radically different as they were from anything else appearing with them in the pages of *The New Yorker*. There is the light-hearted quotation of high modernism played with since his first published story, "Me and Miss Mandible" (in which a protagonist's metamorphosis is not into a repulsive insect but into a gangly and concupiscently riotous sixth grader). As in "The Balloon," another fairly early story, bizarre mechanical intrusions are accepted as commonplace. From "The Viennese Opera Ball" Barthelme revives the practice of running simultaneous stories within the larger narrative line, as bits of information, stock phrases of dialogue, odd mixtures of references, and associations on the level of language combine for a richly stocked (and at times confusingly madcap) story. As in "Florence Green is 81," there is a methodically cubist flatness of plane in which there is no distinction in perspective among the narrative's simultaneous interests; what is real in these storytellings is thereby located on the surface, with readerly attention directed to the page and the action of language upon it (and upon the reader's store of language types, rather than inviting references to an exterior operating world). Information itself is treated as a matter of disjunction; meaning proves to be disruptive when discerned, which encourages the reader to find enjoyment in the easy play of signs rather than searching for what they signify. These early Barthelme stories have content, but often of a type that denies itself by reason, much like a Magritte painting will portray a lamplit city street whose exquisite realistic rendering is contradicted by the brightly sunny sky above. As a result, structure rather than content becomes the focal element, a practice Barthelme would exploit to the fullest in The Dead Father.

It is within the realm of language itself, and not just what language refers to, that Barthelme's novel makes its greatest success. It's an interest the author had shown in Snow White, where his postmodernization of the classic fairy tale / movie consisted of rechoreographing the action into abruptly anachronistic poses, poses which were most often expressed in language (such as the dwarfs speaking like social therapists and phenomenological philosophers, Snow White herself pondering her fate in currently fashionable feminist jargon, and even a national leader expressing himself in the voice and linguistic mannerisms of Lyndon Baines Johnson, president of the United States when this novel was written and published). The technique of taking a rosy-cheeked heroine straight out of Disney or the Grimms and having her speak like Gloria Steinem is a conjunction of opposites, or at least of unlikes, and as such qualifies as the art of collage, a style Barthelme has always believed to be the essence of twentieth-century art. By such juxtapositions, a new reality would be created out of elements which would still retain their original identity—which would have to retain that identity, in fact, for the collage effect to happen. In Snow White, the unlikes retain their identity; although there are three elements rather than two, with both Disney's and the Grimms' features competing with the pop sociology and mod psychology of late 1960s Greenwich Village, the shocking apparency of the last element makes such a great contrast with the first two that the century between the Grimms' work and Disney collapses into a virtual identity that stands in harsh contrast to the she-nanigans played out by the postmodern sides of Barthelme's Snow White and the Seven Dwarfs. Yet even here Barthelme shares kinship with the earlier transcribers, for the Grimms and Disney were also professionals in the business of sign management, the former as folklorists and compara-tive linguists, the latter as a shrewd manipulator of icons within popular culture.

The Dead Father shares this interest in comparing language and consid-ering how signs take place in various cultures, but the facilitating principle of collage is developed further by another technique Barthelme was ob-serving among the younger emerging artists of the 1960s: silkscreen. And it is silkscreening rather than collage that becomes the informing principle of *The Dead Father*. Whereas the basis of collage is the image cut out of one context and repasted in another, as Max Ernst displayed in *Une Semaine de Bonté*, silkscreen expands the catalog of items and permits a photomechani-cal superimposition of elements so that they can bleed through, yielding images seen through one another rather than in simple juxtaposition. Such silkscreening of language may be the hidden key in the strongest of Barthelme's earlier works, such as the story "Report," where weap-onry consists of rots, rusts, and blights capable of attacking the enemy's alphabet and where long-range planning is centered on realtime, online computer-controlled wish evaporation (which, as the narrator explains, is being developed to meet the rising expectations that threaten to exhaust resources). Although elements of collage survive—there are such degen-erative factors as rots and rusts, and there are indeed alphabets—the joke is not in juxtaposing them but in letting each perform an equally valid syntac-tic and referential function within the same smooth phrase. Said quickly and casually enough, the phrase sounds perfectly acceptable, and so rather than using collage's immediate shock of contrast the writer is here planting a clever little time bomb slipped past our censors of the ridiculous. As in silkscreen, the images are superimposed with one bleeding through the other, and in *The Dead Father* Barthelme can be seen using such a technique more deftly than his work with collage in *Snow White*. By the time of *Paradise* his mastery of this style of writing allows him to drop such mechanical techniques altogether and approach his narrative material with language and incident, character and plot alone, yet still achieve results as patently postmodern as any of the period's artists.

There exists within the canon of Donald Barthelme's work a steady movement from apparency to effacement, as the initial starkness of both style and structure yields to a seeming transparency of narration whereby his fictions read like reports about and comments on our commonly shared world. At the same time, the author will draw on certain social subjects—in the case of The Dead Father, Freudian psychology—both for thematic topics and generative techniques. These two features of Barthelme's middle period, centering on The Dead Father but spanning the years between Sadness (1972) and Amateurs (1976), have inspired an interpretation that tries to locate Barthelme's fiction within a larger, more conservative tradition of realism. Yet by considering from whence he had come and especially where his work was taking him, it is possible to see how such transitional elements are only particular factors in the larger import of Barthelme's writing. There is certainly social satire in his short stories, just as psychology proves to be an important interest and even a narratological factor in The Dead Father. But to reduce Barthelme's intent to a mannerist critique of his world or to insist that Lacanian analysis exhausts the creative statement of his second novel misunderstands why the author has chosen these materials in the first place and ignores the way he handles them.

Donald Barthelme's relation to language and what it signifies is first of all as a manipulator of its hard and fast materiality. As a college student at the University of Houston, his interests did not lead him to the usual English major pursuits of poetry and fiction but rather to the offices of the student newspaper, where he worked at such mechanical tasks as makeup and layout. When he did edit stories, it was from the Amusements desk, and the creative work among his student projects consists of satires directed to form (including a take-off on Pilgrim's Progress and another on southern romances replete with a heroine named Amanda Feverish). From the student paper he ridiculed the Houston Post's uninformed opinion that bebop jazz caused gang riots, countering that the swing-and-sway music of bandleader Sammy Kaye was responsible for several mass murders. Yet when graduation took him to the Post as a cub reporter, Barthelme dutifully covered such a potpourri of cultural events as Abbott and Costello's stage show and any number of Doris Day and Walt Disney films. By 1955 Barthelme had accumulated over four hundred such reports, giving him an encyclopedia of American pop culture from which to draw images and events. A listing of these articles reads like a variorum to his fiction; their function is satiric, but more so for their own hard materiality of presence (as on a newspaper's amusements page) rather than as ironic commentary.

Handling words and images as blocks of material rather than as purveyors of conceptions remained Barthelme's job for a decade: in the army as a service newspaper writer, back at the University of Houston as a public relations writer (inspiring a narrator of one later story to recall writing poppycock for the president of a university), and ultimately as the editor of the same school's prestigious quarterly, *Forum*. It was this qualification, in tandem with his other job as director of Houston's Contemporary Arts Museum, that took him to New York to become managing editor of *Location*, an arts and literature journal founded by critics Harold Rosenberg and Thomas Hess. Throughout this first, journalistic stage of his career Barthelme became adept at using language not for reference but for its own sense of performance. As a public relations man, he might be called on not for a searching probe of university assets but rather "a couple hundred words to make the alumni feel generous" or "cool off the regents." As editor of *Forum* and then *Location*, he would publish the most interesting of the new artists, philosophers, and fiction writers of the day—but always with an eye toward page layout, balance of contents, and market image (*Forum* was, after all, essentially a PR vehicle, just as *Location* stood for an image its two founders wished to present and even proselytize). It is this understanding of language—that it often functions in many ways other than for the transmission of ideas, and that in fact its ideas are often in contradiction with the purpose achieved—that becomes the most characteristic initial element of Barthelme's fiction, a body of work that begins appearing almost exactly as his career as a journalist, publicist, and editor comes to a close.

Another facet of his work is shaped by this period, both from his art museum direction in Houston and his editing of *Location* in New York, and that was his familiarity and interaction with the era's new and emerging artists. Although fiction had been slow to discard centuries-old conventions of realism, painting and sculpture had moved from the tradition of an artwork being about something to the postmodern condition of the work being that thing itself, the principle reference being to its own act of creation and existence in performance. In terms of aesthetic philosophy, Harold Rosenberg had theorized this change in his appraisal of the abstract expressionists: that for them the canvas was less a surface upon which to represent than an arena within which to act. His statement accurately described the work of Jackson Pollock, and encompassed styles and practices as various as those of Willem de Kooning, Hans Hofmann, and Franz Kline as well. But the fiction of these same years had yet to make such a transition, as Rosenberg himself complained in the pages of his new magazine. *Location*, by employing Donald Barthelme as managing editor, would hope to stimulate just such discussion and hopefully development by means of a dialogue between art and literature. Thanks to his work in both fields, Barthelme was especially suited for the work. But beyond such editorial responsibilities and mission, he was in a position as a fiction writer to profit uniquely from what he was seeing painted, sculpted, and debated around him. Any consideration of *The Dead Father* and his other novels and short stories, therefore, should consider the influences of and especially affinities with developments in painting and sculpture of the day—one more reason why critical reductions to social satire or Freudian analysis miss the essence of Barthelme's art.

With a layout man's perspective on language and a managing editor's consideration for the use of intellectual discussion, Barthelme spends over a decade devising a new style and form for narrative until, with *The Dead Father*, he is able to compose an artistically complete yet radically postmodern novel. In terms of progressive sequence, it employs the most elementary device of carrying an object through the book from chapter 1 to chapter 23, from point A to point Z, as the dead father is dragged from his position in life to his ultimate place of rest in the grave. The cast of characters is similarly limited: the father, his son, two young women, and nineteen men in the hauling party, making a total of twenty-three persons to match the number of chapters (when the action pauses for a framed narrative, the "Manual for Sons" within chapter 17, it too has twenty-three subdivisions, a reminder that the author is being painstakingly particular in his symmetrical minimalism).

Within such stark and orderly limitations, Barthelme uses language itself to expand *The Dead Father* into the larger dimensions of a novel. Whereas his short stories are often demonstrations (and therefore accomplishments) of a particular thematic or technical point (the dissonance of competing sign systems in "Miss Mandible," the bevy of actions on a single plane in "Florence Green," the clever plays in "Report"), this novel, so central to his career, brings all such points into play to serve a larger purpose: sustaining and deepening a narrative whose generative force consumes rather than merely amuses the reader. If a short story is a moment, then a novel is a world, and showing how such a world can be accomplished within the peculiar aesthetic of postmodernism, where fiction is not supposed to be about something but should rather be that thing itself, is what *The Dead Father* achieves.

The Dead Father, then, stands at the center of Donald Barthelme's too short life. It is his totally idiosyncratic work, encompassing everything from his most specific writerly techniques to his mode of humor with his wife, acquaintances, and hapless waiters—all of which reveal their own generative force by boomeranging back in his (or his reader's) face. It is socially pertinent and artistically abstract, fragmentedly pointed yet grandly narrative in its sweep. *The Dead Father* suggests the text that Donald Barthelme created for his life, and which makes for a life of fiction even as that vitality questions itself (or is challenged by one's wife and the reputation of one's father). Larger than any one interpretation of his art, it encompasses all of them, and suggests what Barthelme's fiction is all about.

Chapter One

Early Fiction as Technique

The object known as the Dead Father being hauled across the land-scape in Donald Barthelme's novel can be almost anything or anybody one wishes. Like all symbols, it is at once a natural father (with any number of socially accurate touches of typical behavior, often quite funny ones) and everything fatherhood implies (from the father's need to dominate to his son's apparent need to be dominated). Yet there is sufficient allegory in this character's execution that the figure suggests meanings from the world of art and philosophy as well. In terms such as these, the Dead Father represents an older, passing order, one whose statements and actions conflict with the very manner in which it is presented. By exploiting both substance and form, Barthelme manages to satirize an aesthetic philosophy even as he presents it, making The Dead Father be something even as it undertakes being about a certain topic.

Widely recognized as pioneering an innovative fictive style commonly and loosely described as postmodern, Barthelme uses the occasion of his second novel to carry modernism to its grave. Although the Dead Father never announces the issue as such, the questioning of modernist beliefs stands behind most of the obstacles he encounters; and if feminism can be considered a postmodern development, then its announcement in the text makes the aesthetic conflict all the more explicit. But most apparent is the author's attitude toward modernist themes and conventions, at times whimsical and almost always wryly ironic. It is as if Samuel Beckett were to rewrite his dramatic masterpiece to give Godot both a stage presence and spoken lines wildly inappropriate to the dialogue undertaken by Vladimir and Estragon. Yet as Ihab Hassan has explained, the first generation of postmodernists preferred to write a literature of silence, and therefore Vladimir and Estragon's questions go unanswered while Godot himself stays out of the picture. Half an age later it will be Donald Barthelme who brings him back to show how radically things have changed.

From the start of his fictionist's career, which begins with short stories in 1961 and a first collection in 1964, Barthelme has taken a satirical stance toward literary modernism. Indeed, some critics have argued that this is all he does, using the conventional forms of parody and ridicule to engage the modern on its own terms. Yet distinctions must be drawn, including the subjects of his attacks and the form those critiques take. As targets, the foibles of high modernism are just that: not deep-reaching issues capable of sustaining an artistic work, but rather easily caricaturized sacred cows with which the text has unabashed fun. The purpose is more to signal an attitude than engage a serious debate, for Barthelme's argument with modernism takes place on the level of form, not content. Here the satirized object, already having set a mood of irreverence in terms of topical reference, functions formally by virtue of appearing egregiously out of context and being asked to do something wildly inappropriate to its presumed stature. When the Dead Father issues ukases like an obsolescent czar or rages in a fit of slaying—all because of a perceived sexual slight—he not only seems out of place, but throws into high relief the contrary doings of his postcontemporaries (notably his son who more comfortably accepts a less dominant role and the women who are devising an entirely new order of gender). Seen broadly, *The Dead Father* is only linear, serial, and developmental in its narrative so that these contrary presences—modern and postmodern—can disrupt such conventional structure by their rival strivings. There is something more important occurring in the work than satiric commentary on the father's silliness and his picaresque progress toward the grave.

That importance can be understood by looking back to Barthelme's earliest stories, where attitudes toward modernism and its aftermath provide the spark to get the young man going as a writer. His first published fiction, following an early career in journalism, public relations, journal editing, and the directing of a contemporary arts museum (all of which contribute topics, attitudes, and techniques to his subsequent work), was a story in the seventh number of a little magazine called *Contact* (February 1961, pp. 17–28), "The Darling Duckling at School." Collected three years later in *Come Back, Dr. Caligari* as "Me and Miss Mandible," the piece is catalyzed by the irreverent move of taking the Kafkaesque premise of having a protagonist awake suddenly in bizarrely transformed circumstances and be sentenced to live out the quotidian progress of life in this horribly uncomfortable shape. As men, Kafka's and Barthelme's figures are much the same: discomforted, betrayed, and anxiously ill at ease not only with their new circumstances but with the apparent meaninglessness of their condition. But it is in the particulars of those conditions that the modern and postmodern authors diverge, for while Kafka's Gregor Samsa is turned into a literal insect, Barthelme's unfortunate is a thirty-five-year-old insurance adjustor inexplicably returned to the adolescently overheated confines of a sixth grade classroom, where he plays an only partially unwilling part in a fantasized love triangle among himself, his teacher, and the eleven-year-old girl across the aisle.

Barthelme's story is, of course, parodic, for it could hardly exist without Kafka's paradigm in the past—or even more so, as a structure placed canonically within our present circumstances of reading and writing. Yet the piece is much more than this, since from Kafka it looks to the present for further paradigms, including not only the common psychological ploy of a borderline pubescent boy learning the fascinations of sexuality by dreaming about his teacher but the analogue from the day's popular culture (significantly enough in adult magazines the school children can only partly comprehend), such as the luridly publicized romantic triangle of Debbie Reynolds, Eddie Fisher, and Elizabeth Taylor. If the structure is already there in Kafka's story, the roles are equally tailor-made in the world of fan magazines, where the children match up with the cute young lovers while Miss Mandible evokes the threatening maturity of the veteran actress.

This succession of paradigms suggests a Chinese box effect, implying that not only is Barthelme's story within Kafka's, but that the Eddie and Debbie saga lies within the newer writer's own set piece. By doing so is the author simply satirizing or parodying modernism, effecting a theft which by virtue of imitation flatters what it ridicules and is, in any case, crafted solidly within the original type? If parody were the only purpose, the answer would be yes. But looking further, one finds that "Me and Miss Mandible" is up to something entirely different from Kafka's tale of metamorphosis. The experience Gregor Samsa undergoes is central to the modernist ethic: he is the quintessential antihero, alienated from his context yet forced to live within it, anxiously questioning the reason for such existence even as it tolls out the hours of his fate. His is a typically absurd situation, and Kafka's narrative art fashions every detail of it to highlight such judgment for the reader. Barthelme's insurance adjustor shares all of these features and conditions; yet whereas for Kafka they were the essence of his story, Barthelme uses them only as a beginning. True, he can take advantage of Kafka's intertextual presence in the minds of readers and most likely within any fiction a subsequent author might write. But from this beginning "Me and Miss Mandible" proceeds in a remarkably different direction. Free of overweening anxiety and not painfully dedicated to existential questioning or angst, it rather accepts the premise as a given of life in this world. As modernists have proved, things like this can happen, and Barthelme has no argument with the context. What one does with this text is another question, and within the manner by which he proceeds one can see how Barthelme makes something quite new of what for Kafka had been a terminal situation.

If the characters in both stories seem helpless, there is at least an answer for it in "Me and Miss Mandible." Existence may in each case seem incomprehensible; but given what Barthelme's protagonist knows about adolescent life and the education level of sixth grade, he can analyze the problem and propose an answer. Gregor Samsa looks at his world and finds its interpretation vexed by problems of meaning; his suspicion, confirmed by ultimate modernist belief, is that it is meaningless. Barthelme's character is similarly puzzled with his situation, being moved back two dozen years into this grade school classroom, but he never once ascribes his condition to meaninglessness. Instead, there are meanings all around— too many of them, too easily merchandised and consumed. Answers that Gregor Samsa may have sought are here supplied like consumer goods in a supermarket, and rather than searching in a void for something quite undefined Barthelme's protagonist and his classmates are deluged with the surfeit of interpretations, all of which are packaged as neat little texts that stock the larger narratives of their lives.

The meanings of texts are deciphered by reading, and reading is one of the subjects school children are still studying in sixth grade. The advantage Barthelme's thirty-five year old has is that he is a past master of reading, while his classmates may still be struggling with the meanings of certain arcane or polysyllabic words. Even more than technical expertise, the man also has the advantage of experience, for his two decades of adult life out in the real world have taught him something that will never appear in the curriculum short of a doctoral seminar on postmodernism itself: "that signs are signs, and that some of them are lies" (CB, p. 109). This is, in fact, the lesson confirmed by his return to sixth grade, where he sees his colleagues struggling to interpret everything from fan magazine stories to the subtextual relationship between teacher and student, female and male, adult and child.

There is an irony in both stories, but whereas the modernist writer is deadly serious even with patently comic materials, the postmodern writer cannot help but take the situation tongue-in-cheek. "Plucked from my unexamined life among other pleasant, desperate, money-making young Americans," Barthelme's narrator notes, "thrown backward in space and time, I am beginning to understand how I went wrong," and he is unable to resist adding the phrase that skewers high modern seriousness, "how we all go wrong" (CB, p. 108)—spoken by a thirty-five year old squeezed into the sixth grade desk. His questioning winds up being silly, because Barthelme's sensibility—fresh as a fiction writer but tempered by nearly ten years' work in the manufacture of serviceable prose—knows that probing for something behind a sign is a waste of time. Better to appreciate the texture of signification itself, which is what his narrator learns to do by savoring the systematics of the Reynolds-Fisher-Taylor relationship (characterized by seventeen "Eddie and Debbie" headlines listed in the manner used so well in The Dead Father) and having more fun reading the intentionality of Sue Ann Brownly and Miss Mandible than being troubled by the substance of their rivalry (which, given Sue Ann's prepubescent status, has no real substance at all).

And so Barthelme's initially parodic appropriation of one of Kafka's great themes becomes much more than simple parody. The irreverently comic attitude toward the older writer's device of transformation deflates it of seriousness and thereby relieves any overbearing anxiety of influence. Yet the technique is cited (and employed) just the same, granting Barthelme's work a multidimensionality that both incorporates Kafka's range and reaches farther, in this case toward an ability to experience not just the text's narration but also the reading of it. In this way a tenet of literary modernism is both used and critiqued, taking a practice once held to be an end in itself (proclaiming the lack of meaning) and employing it to take another step beyond—one that both reflects back on modernism and, by using it to do something else, contradicts it.

It takes the ease of comedy to slip the reader into this new style of self-generating activity. Instead of the horror and dread instilled by Kafka's vision, we are given the amusing posturings of Barthelme's narrator, who begins his journal with a sentence as startling as anything in Kafka, but which—in the unwinding of the carefully constructed paragraph that follows—defuses the volatility of his first line while at the same time establishing a context for the equally unlikely phrase that concludes it:

> *13 September*
>
> Miss Mandible wants to make love to me but she hesitates because I am officially a child. I am, according to the records, according to the gradebook on her desk, according to the card index in the principal's office, eleven years old. There is a misconception here, one that I haven't quite managed to get cleared up yet. I am in fact thirty-five, I've been in the Army, I am six feet one, I have hair in the appropriate places, my voice is a baritone, I know very well what to do with Miss Mandible if she ever makes up her mind. (CB, p. 97)

From the typically modernist shock of unreason, the protagonist takes us to the candidly postmodern raunchiness of his closing admission, with the contrasts in both content and style graduated by the details protested in between. In this manner the reader is invited to participate on the level of sign recognition rather than direct conceptualization, for that initial sentence demands a shared appreciation of how many narratives from the era of high modernism depended on such effect, whereas the enumeration of evidence (from statistics of birth and military service to explicit signs of sexual maturity) takes subtle but progressive steps toward the bold frankness of his concluding proposition, in itself the most obvious proof that he has indeed matured. In this process, the initial threat of unreason is replaced by a more accommodating notion of sexual enjoyment; what is at first a hideous suggestion, sex between an adult and a child, is transformed into a reasonable prospect, its expressive language overcoming the physical limitations of the story's first-reported transformation.

Even as the narrative moves on to report the sixth grade class's struggles with signs and meanings (as they read forbidden copies of Movie-TV Secrets and puzzle over its sexual gossip and ads for boudoir apparel), the narrator keeps subverting his tale with insertions of contextually inappropriate language. He cannot describe the seating plan without noting, of Sue Ann Brownly across from him, that she is, "like Miss Mandible, a fool for love" (CB, p. 97). His psychological analysis returns to this notion: "The distinction between children and adults, while probably useful for some purposes, is at bottom a specious one, I feel. There are only individual egos, crazy for love" (CB, p. 108). Longer entries detailing action in class are contrasted with the occasional single-sentence reminders of the Kafkaesque predicament, such as "30 October: I return again and again to the problem of my future" (CB, p. 104). Yet the future is just what is being promised to these youngsters, and all of them except the narrator can accept it with blithe innocence. It is obvious to him that "the sixth grade at Horace Greeley Elementary is a furnace of love, love, love" (CB, p. 106), and given his prospects for satisfaction, there is no real reason to break out. "Here I am safe," he admits, "I have a place; I do not wish to entrust myself once more to the whimsy of authority" (CB, p. 107). And so the conventionally modernist theme of striving to break out of such a prison is transformed to the more postmodern notion of going with the flow and appreciating the texture of existence as provided. When he and Miss Mandible finally complete their tryst, he is as happy as an adult, yet as safe as a child. As for Sue Ann Brownly, who discovers them, she is the one who grows up, having been taught how to read, "certain now which of us was Debbie, which Eddie, which Liz" (CB, p. 110).

As Donald Barthelme's first published story, "Me and Miss Mandible" promises much of what will be developed in his style by the time of *The Dead Father* fourteen years later. In addition to the specifically postmodern use of modernist themes and techniques, and beyond the deflationary tactic of spoofing his predecessors' high seriousness, we see the author learning how refreshing it can be to alternate rhythms of action and analysis within the larger strategy of questioning the very substance of his narrative. Such questioning, offered so seriously by Kafka, becomes in postmodern hands something that the reader will never take as seriously as the narrator. And even the narrator seems to be setting things up for comic effect—never participating in the joke, but deadpanning his way through in a manner that exploits the contextual possibility of the page. In the Miss Mandible story, thick passages of recounted action contrast with single-line entries, with the narrator's diary format emphasizing this contrast on the printed page. *The Dead Father* uses a similar layout of thick and thin, with the relatively complete interpolations of action set off against one- or two-word sentences ranked in single file just like the crew of men hauling the immense carcass. Simply moving back and forth between these modes is pleasant and relieving, factors Kafka would have found foreign to his own narrative but which Barthelme delights in for their sake of multiplicity and plurality, reminding us that there is no one interpretation the author is pounding home. Rather "Me and Miss Mandible," like *The Dead Father*, presents a variety of contextual experiences, the point of which often resides in the texture of shifts and contrasts.

In terms of conventional appreciation, such shifts in attention are disruptions of the normal process of understanding, if understanding a piece of fiction consists in conceptualizing its meaning. One of Barthelme's departures from tradition is to relocate meaning within context and texture, asking his readers to look away from the previously central concerns of character and plot in order to sense the more subtle aspects of his art. Here is where the greater sweep of stories in *Come Back, Dr. Caligari* indicates the parameters of his writing that will be exploited so fully in *The Dead Father*. "Me and Miss Mandible" turns out to be one of the more orderly pieces in terms of form, for its progression is linear, chronological, and accumulative in terms of meaning. Many other stories in the volume are not, abandoning such integral factors in order to achieve other effects that make their own contribution to the style of fiction that will ultimately mature in Barthelme's second novel so many years later.

Initially most disconcerting for readers who in 1964 discovered this new book popping up amid the regularities and confirmed expectations of story collections by Updike, O'Hara, and Cheever were the multiplicity of nonsequential narrative lines within individual short fictions by this new writer just recently arrived from Houston yet as urbanely polished as a lifetime Greenwich Villager. The second shock, surely part of the author's intended effect, is to find that these disruptions of sequence are themselves complex matters: not just separately divisive topics, but narrative lines themselves disrupted by apparently random information, second and third stories, and references to entirely different things. Placed next to "Me and Miss Mandible" and the other structurally conventional stories from Dr. Caligari (a total of six from fourteen), such apparently disorganized selections as "Florence Green is 81" and "The Viennese Opera Ball," occupying the beginning and middle of the collection, shake up the initial setting of Barthelme's own oeuvre, inviting readers to wonder if this young writer is still searching for a style. Yet the same seeming disparities of method are evident within the single and full-length work, The Dead Father, requiring a critical explanation. The fact is that this apparent diversity of method is central to the author's purpose in breaking up the modernist lock on expression and interpretation, from the unrelieved monological seriousness overthrown in "Miss Mandible" to the prolificacy of independent actions in "Florence Green." In two cases Barthelme's explosions of themes and forms take place within individual stories: the catalog of Batman jokes in "The Joker's Greatest Triumph" and the marginal glosses accompanying the action of "To London and Rome," techniques which relocate the stories' action from their flimsy, single-joke plots to the more abundant activity on the page itself. The stories collected in Dr. Caligari, representing almost the author's entire output during his four years in the trade (a few short satires would appear later in Guilty Pleasures, a volume initially set apart from his short story canon), are dedicated to nothing less than reinventing the modes for writing and reading within this most traditional of domains, and so it should not be surprising to see Barthelme using an exceptionally wide range of techniques. What is remarkable, and demands close study, is how those diverse techniques turn out not to be a broadly scattershot approach to literary revolution but establish the sustained integrity of a novel in *The Dead Father*.

With *Come Back, Dr. Caligari*, the first question to ask is what remains in common among the traditionally structured, transitionally organized, and overtly fragmentary stories Donald Barthelme has crafted between 1961 and 1964. Of the simpler, more direct pieces, most rely on a single effect, often a satirically thematic attack on some pretension of high modernism. Complementing the whimsical critique of Kafkaesque brooding in "Me and Miss Mandible" is the direct quotation of modernism's central poem in "Marie, Marie, Hold on Tight." This line from T. S. Eliot's *The Waste Land* does not figure in the narrative but rather, as title, sets the tone for it. The story's business itself concerns a group of men dedicated to answering what may well be Eliot's question in that section of his poem: why does the human condition have to be the way it is? Their protest, however, takes on the same whimsy that characterizes "Me and Miss Mandible," a comic approach that prevents an overly serious emphasis on theme from detracting from the story's true emphasis, which is on the play of technique. Marie, as in Eliot's poem, appears only as the object of direct address, itself an interesting variation in the narrative's sense of person—for while nearly all of the story is told from a limited omniscient point of view (from among the participants, with the narrator never personally identified), occasional parenthetical remarks are directed to her by name. She has painted the protest signs and stands behind them in a position to be proud. But she is hardly a character herself, and therefore her remarked presence in the piece serves to evoke Eliot's line, even though the words themselves appear only in the title.

The premise itself is simple but comically penetrating in terms of surprising aptness: as others picket city, state, and specific businesses and industry for redress of grievances, Barthelme's three men stage their protest against the human condition in front of a church, a theological definition being their idea of the problem's root. Their signs themselves are not only funny in themselves, but their messages—parodic parallels of what irate taxpayers or striking steam fitters complain about to those responsible—present the author with another chance to list phrases on the page, such as the eight lines of block capitals reminiscent of the Eddie-and-Debbie headlines in "Miss Mandible." Again, the nature of their action is transformed from a vague idea into a concrete presence on the page, something the structure of *The Dead Father* will do on several occasions. These block typefaces contrast with the otherwise conventional linearity of the story, adding a spatial dimension that the thematic action picks up quite easily, as in the contrast between the protestors' action and the bypassers' response:

> Henry Mackie repeated that belief was not involved, and said that it was, rather, a question of man helpless in the grip of a definition of himself that he had not drawn, that could not be altered by human action, and that was in fundamental conflict with every human notion of what should obtain. The pickets were simply subjecting this state of affairs to a radical questioning, he said.
>
> "You're putting me on," the youth said, and attempted to kick Henry Mackie in the groin. (CB, p. 121)

From the posters, which state such things as THE SOUL IS NOT! and REMEMBER YOU ARE DUST!, Barthelme's narrative moves into not just a consideration of content but an exercise in form, as the story line itself (not a direct quote) assumes the cast of philosophical language—specifically, the style of inquiry made famous by the great modernist thinkers from Kierkegaard on down. Next, to show how odd this language looks when thrust into the world of daily affairs, a bystander steps in with his own words, jarringly contradicting the protestor's style and adding some physical emphasis to go with it. Thematically, then, "Marie, Marie, Hold on Tight" begins with an evidently simple premise—hardly enough to sustain a story—but from there proceeds to build itself on the level of language, which is an entirely different realm of action. Modernist concerns are not simply satirized in theme and content but are supplanted in terms of technique by shifting attention from thought to words.

Much of the doings in *The Dead Father* are there for similar purpose, with Barthelme taking his action out of the way in order to bring in the physical presence of language. The inscription itself is the central point of "Margins," another relatively simple tale from this first collection that derives its effect not just from an arrestingly odd thematic statement but from the expression of that theme in a distinctive technical manner. A hand-writing analysis book is employed to define character, directing attention to the page even more emphatically than in the previous stories. And not just handwriting, but the margins surrounding it on the page—an equally physical context for inscribed language. Thus the page takes on a reality quite apart from conceptual content; or at the very least, the physical presence of stylistically executed language reveals more than the words' references themselves. The story's action is little more than a dialogue between the one character who proposes to solve everything through handwriting analysis and another whose mission is to decry his fate by printing it out and parading it on sandwich boards. "*I was Put In Jail in Selby County Alabama For Five Years For Stealing A Dollar And A Half Which I Did Not Do,*" the first line reads, followed by others which compound the injustice but also turn into a rote litany of such fates, until the message ends as a formula itself, "*Patent Applied For & Deliver Us From Evil*" (CB, p. 142). From these promptings, the discussion can never rise from its inscribed surface, the second man only able to continue by quizzing his colleague about books he's read (never going beyond author and title), the first man reaching no further depth of inquiry (or understanding) than to ask if he really didn't steal that dollar and a half. The resolution is the first's advice to the second to concentrate on improving his handwriting. "My character, you mean," he asks, and is told "No . . . don't bother improving your character. Just improve your handwriting. Make larger capitals. Make smaller loops in your 'y' and your 'g.' Watch your word-spacing so as not to display disorientation. Watch your margins" (CB, p. 146). The lesson from "Miss Mandible" is recalled, that signs are signs; some of them may be lies, but signs (and not meanings) are what are read, and since all inferences derive from that reading, one should make sure of the signs first (and perhaps also last) of all.

Protest signs reading as if written by Søren Kierkegaard or Frederick Douglass (whose writings occupy our consciousness like signboards from our schooling), lists of abstract qualities or headline phrases ranked like so many items in a supermarket (from which we choose in composing the larger texts of our lives), narrative actions that seem much more like the rummagings in a library for writing a research paper, or a survey of the material littering the public relations releases, catalog descriptions, and journalistic critiques of our times—these are the materials from which Barthelme forms his fiction, thematically satirizing their unquestioned seriousness within the modernist aesthetic even as he turns that system inside out by reversing its values and functions. Some of his earliest short stories are single-issue exercises in this direction, not coming together for an integrated and sustained action until the maturity of The Dead Father. But their contiguity as an artistically assembled collection suggests an overall effect anticipating the later novel, and it is important to note that the volume's organization takes a radical departure from the stories' order of first publication, and that some of its most complex pieces are among the earliest written. As an author moving to New York and enjoying a supportive relationship with such a prestigious magazine as The New Yorker, Barthelme seems to begin with many of his talents already in hand, the limits of the short story form dictating their division among the various parts that do not coalesce until four years' work is brought together in a volume such as Dr. Caligari.

Consider how the lighter stories are scattered throughout the volume, with the protest signs and sandwich boards of "Marie" and "Margins" waiting until two-thirds through, just where too much unrelieved seriousness or heavy technical experiment might bog down a reading. Similarly, the jokes on topical matters (the dullness of Cleveland in "Up, Aloft in the Air," the peculiarities of the national anthem in "The Big Broadcast of 1938," the batty intricacies of European philosophy in "A Shower of Gold," the ghastly shallowness of the couple in "Will You Tell Me?") are spread out across the collection's beginning, middle, and end, insuring the book's essentially comic nature even as some very sophisticated formal challenges are undertaken along the way.

In terms of more serious disruption, no less than half a dozen of the volume's fourteen stories address themselves to specific conventions that, unchallenged, would leave Barthelme's art in relatively traditional form. In "The Piano Player" a familiar tale of wifely discontent is exaggerated by making the woman's string of typically uxorial complaints linguistically (rather than realistically) based, in turn highlighting what will become a regular feature of Barthelme's work (and a prominent part of The Dead Father): portraying the male in his role of husband and father as beleaguered to the point of having the very foundations of his world in reason and language undermined. Here the protagonist has to face her complaint that "I'm ugly. . . . Our children are ugly" and listen to a list of problems indicative of much more than a bad day in the kitchen:

> "The ham died," she said. "I couldn't cure it. I tried everything. You don't love me any more. The penicillin was stale. I'm ugly and so are the children. It said to tell you goodbye." (CB, p. 19)

As the narrative continues, complaints mount, steady in frequency but increasingly bizarre in terms of substance. "The giraffe is on fire, but I don't suppose you care," the wife accuses, and within the page adds that "you've got to get me an air hammer. To clean the children's teeth. What's the name of that disease? They'll all have it, every single one, if you don't get me an air hammer" (CB, p. 22). The giraffe is straight from Salvador Dali; the air hammer for the kids' teeth seems out of a sequential collage by Max Ernst. But although the individual materials are modernist—classically modernist, in fact—Barthelme's intent is quite different from the surrealists'. "The Piano Player" is no dreamscape or land of nightmare distortions; instead, it is in all but a very few accidentals our own world, upon which, to anticipate his title for a later story, Barthelme undertakes a critique de la vie quotidienne in which the emphasis is clearly on daily life. The giraffe and the air hammer are not integral elements of the composition, as in Dali and Ernst, but rather iconic references to modernism itself, the mechanical insertion of which underscores the bland predictability of these characters' dully suburban life style. "The Piano Player" depends most of all on timing; its actions move forward with an almost plodding regularity, and when an outstanding reference to modernist distortion threatens to intervene, the story's steady ongoing rhythm quickly effaces it by drawing it into the routine. No matter how startling the object, the wife subsumes it into her steadily paced complaint—the air hammer is just an incidental to the horrors of periodontics and the struggle to keep the children's teeth healthy and straight, the combustible giraffe just one more instance of her husband not caring. Thanks to our thorough education in modernism, Dali and Ernst are forever present in our lives as intertextual elements. But Barthelme's emphasis is on postmodern life and its dominant rhythms, rhythms which can chew up and swallow the most horrific of high modern images like so much breakfast toast.

Just the opposite technique works to the same effect in "Hiding Man." Here several different sign systems are recognized as such. The narrative is generated by their differences, in fact, but the protagonist's role is not just to experience them but to make a thorough integration of their distinctive parts. The situation is a simple one: the character enters a cheap and somewhat sinister movie house, empty but for one other person, a well-dressed but vaguely threatening presence (dark glasses, different race) who is watching both the cinema's typical fare (third-rate horror films with preposterous premises) and anyone who may enter. Within this most basic of circumstances Barthelme expands the action by drawing attention to the sign systems behind these diverse features, the one thing they have in common.

Everything is primarily a message, and the task is to read. On coming across someone whose signs suggest possible hostility, the protagonist looks for an exit, but even its sign is ambiguous (bulb out, no real proof that it is a secure escape). There is some debate as to whether the theater is open (it rarely has an audience greater than one or two, and the other character claims a "closed" sign is posted on the door). The films themselves depend on signs rather than actual presences, "all superior examples of genre, tending toward suggested offscreen rapes, obscene tortures: man with huge pliers advancing on disheveled beauty, cut to girl's face, to pliers, to man's face, to girl, scream, blackout" (CB, p. 25). The existence of the film the two men watch, *Attack of the Puppet People*, cannot be defined in itself but only by reference to the system within which it exists: *Cool and the Crazy, She Gods of Shark Reef, Night of the Blood Beast, Diary of a High School Bride,* and *Circus of Horrors.* As the story proceeds, each reference to the film onscreen invokes the titles of still other films, always recounted in lists. When the characters finally begin a conversation, it soon devolves into listing of items, as when a reference to childhood religion generates a page-long list of materials and practices from Catholicism. The effect is a clear one: that the characters and their narrative actions have their own life within systematics, the real references thereof never figuring in any matters of consequence. In the company of "The Piano Player," "Hiding Man" establishes the contextual mode of Barthelme's fiction. For him, references are never things in themselves, be they burning giraffes or horror films. Rather, one surrealistic device is an index to the existence of all others, just as it is impossible for a single fright movie to exist without its characterizing genre. Yet there are still ample opportunities for narrative, since reading these signs and drawing on the library from which they come can provide endless activity—which may be indeed what life is about.

In common among the stories discussed so far is a shift of both writerly and readerly energy from the depth of meaning to the surface of signification. The purpose is not to say that meaning (or, for the modernists, meaninglessness) is unimportant, but rather to establish how there is abundantly interesting action on the surface, and that here indeed is where the business of being human takes place. What Barthelme's diverse techniques share is a commitment to those systematics; from spoofs of modernist themes to unflappable rhythms and interminable lists, his surprisingly new methods are all dedicated to this flattery and enjoyment of the surface.

"The Piano Player" and "Hiding Man" dramatize this process, but other equally direct stories make additional contributions to Barthelme's aesthetic. "For I'm the Boy Whose Only Joy Is Loving You," published in the magazine for which he himself was the managing editor, is a straightforward monologue, displaying the author's talents for characterized speech and linguistic drama—another reminder of how interesting the surface of language can be (the narrative itself has no great drama or even action). "Up, Aloft in the Air" seems to exist for making jokes, in this case at the expense of what the narrative presumes to be the colorless, banal cities of Ohio. The joking itself is feeble, and like "For I'm the Boy . . ." there is not a great deal of interesting action (the story was never separately published, appearing first in *Come Back, Dr. Caligari*, one of its jokes giving the volume its name). But how the jokes are made is the work's redeeming factor, as Barthelme with seeming nonchalance tosses off one liners that undertake the most amazing transformations of language. There are, for example, "the exotic instruments of Cleveland, the dolor, the mangle, the bim" (CB, p. 128); another town, famed for its rubber tire industry, boasts "a wine of the region, a light Cheer" (CB, p. 132); and the medical society of Toledo is counted off in a list that runs from "Dr. Caligari / Dr. Frank / Dr. Pepper / Dr. Scholl" (CB, p. 134) to several cartoon, storybook, and television characters. In these cases the humor is not just in the zaniness of the terms selected, but from the way our own knowledge of their sources yields a sense of systems run amuck. Pneumatic tires and a local wine might very well suggest the taste of laundry detergent, but the musical instruments are a more complex matter: *dolor* is an emotional state, a *mangle* is part of an old-fashioned washing machine's wringer, but—having been prompted to trace and associate meanings—what is a *bim*? In similar manner, the doctors listed from Toledo tease one's sense of meaning: one is a famous doctor from the German movie, another from a soap opera on TV; a third is a brand name for corn plasters, but what is the connection to the Dr. Pepper we know as a soft drink? Propelled among familiar systems of reference, we are challenged to investigate meaning on a new level— not just the author's own odd combinations, but the previously unquestioned allusions (such as this name for a carbonated beverage) from our everyday world.

Within this fresh attention to systems of meanings rather than to meanings themselves, which are surely less interesting and less fun, Barthelme builds a context for strikingly lyrical language. "The rubbery smell of Akron, sister city of Lahore, Pakistan, lay like the flameout of all our hopes over the plateau that evening" (CB, p. 129), a subsection of his story begins. On the other hand, an amusing little story such as "The Joker's Greatest Triumph," which builds itself almost entirely on a vitalized inventory of Batman paraphernalia, shifts from its rhythm of staccato one liners to feature a long and involved paragraph extolling the Joker's features, its wealth of details couched lovingly in a rhetorical display of balanced periods and parallel constructions. "That's extremely well said," the auditor admits, only to be told "I was paraphrasing what Mark Schorer said about Sinclair Lewis" (CB, p. 157). In similar manner, a column of glosses in "To London and Rome" allows the narrator to comment on his own story even as it develops in the more conventional right-hand column. For all of these examples, relatively simple tales have served as chances for Barthelme to shift an action from a traditional mode, where it would be unexceptional, to a previously untried level, that of signification itself, where the most routine doings now take on a thrilling atmosphere of discovery. During these same years Roland Barthes was delighting French readers with fresh discoveries among the most familiar of daily objects, from washday product packaging to fan magazine photography, showing how what was always assumed to be true is in fact a most arbitrary construction. Such demonstrations were not intended to be profound unmaskings of meaning, but rather clever reminders of just how fascinating the process is. The stories of Come Back, Dr. Caligari are from this same world, a world just uncovering the magic of how things work. And like a child with a new toy, Barthelme plays this fascination in all directions, making even the most modest story an exercise in revelation.

This delight in play, exposing the workings of a system for its own sense of wonder and also as a lesson about how freshly interesting could be something that others had dismissed as deadeningly familiar, makes the Barthelme of Dr. Caligari a kindred spirit with the Barthes of Mythologies and The Eiffel Tower. For each, there is a multiplicity of interest that never dissipates into a pluralism of intent; instead, both writers range far and wide to bring the reader back from such a whirlwind and even madcap journey to see that one specific point has been ever in mind. Barthes' reading of the Eiffel Tower works this way, a paragraph beginning with one aspect of the structure and then reaching out to include the whole city, yet concluding with a line that brings the initial sentiment home to the reader, who has now been concretely involved. A similar range distinguishes The Dead Father, which uses the listing technique of "Up, Aloft in the Air," the impertinent sexual references of "Me and Miss Mandible," and the rhythmic pacings of "The Piano Player" in a style of writing that flatters the built-in readership qualities of "Hiding Man." Yet within the Dr. Caligari collection are stories that themselves draw on this diversity of method and present a range of actions and techniques that anticipate Barthelme's novel at its best.

Each of his collections will include at least a story or two pushing his readers to a new plateau of ability. As Kurt Vonnegut has remarked, the author's regular appearance in The New Yorker over such a long and steady span allowed readers to get to know how to read him, much like a symphony working with a gifted composer and learning how to perform his or her works. For fiction, the readers are the performers, and the plan of Barthelme's first collection sets out an exercise in readerly technique. Its two most innovatively complex stories, "Florence Green Is 81" and "The Viennese Opera Ball," do everything and more than the simpler individual works spread throughout the volume. Surprisingly, "Florence Green" comes first, surely alarming the conservatively trained reader of 1964 (when the form's standard was set by John O'Hara and younger masters such as John Updike were still relatively new to audiences). But then there are five much simpler stories, their techniques parceled out in more easily handled form, before "The Viennese Opera Ball" appears to congratulate readers on how much they can now appreciate as the norm.

The most obvious feature of the first piece is the narrative's commitment to a flat cubist plane. Like perspectives in a Picasso portrait, several stories are presented simultaneously, with no distinction in view. This practice at once slows down the reader, making it impossible to digest the prose at the same speed as a newspaper feature. Likewise, the reader's habitual attempt to accumulate and deduce meaning is frustrated, for the successive segments of "Florence Green Is 81" refuse to yield little nuggets of sense. Instead, where the reader expects a sensible transition, Barthelme makes a fragmentary leap, and where logic suggests a parallel, the reader is confronted with no apparent rhetorical relationship at all.

The more one struggles to impose a rhetoric, the more Barthelme's materials resist it. Within a few pages the reader is deconditioned, or is at least in no position to do much more than surrender to the story's apparently random form. Now, with the inclination to look toward an external standard of reference no longer a factor, the narrative can rest securely on the page—just as Picasso would have settled his viewer's vision on the flat surface of the canvas, all to show how much more can be accomplished there without the need of venturing out for meanings. Offered instead is the rich presence of action on the page, a world in place without the limiting constraints of reason, constraints which Michel Foucault has shown mask and modify to human and not natural purpose.

Not that "Florence Green" lacks meaning. From its first lines the story is fraught with it, as the characters surrounding old Florence struggle to interpret her desire to go to a different country. Yet when information comes, it is disjunctive rather than consequential, reminding readers how

insubstantial and certainly inconclusive the narrative has been. The process can be seen in the initial lines of this story, the first of which sets
the occasion (dinner with Florence Green, in just those words), the second reporting her strange desire, the third recounting the guests' wonder,
the fourth giving no answer but instead letting Florence fall asleep at the
table. With the fifth sentence Barthelme's narrative begins a new but presumably connected development, as the narrator notes the confusion of
a young woman seated next to Florence and gives her a reassuring look.
The look, however, is quoted parenthetically, "a look that says, 'There is
nothing to worry about, I will explain everything later in the privacy of
my quarters Kathleen,'" and from here the story's logical thread begins to
unravel. The reader might be inclined to accept this as a typical twist of the
mystery tale, a spooky new development, pregnant with meaning yet to be
explained but which can be counted on to resolve all questions later. However, there is no such path to be pursued. Instead, a sixth sentence appears
from nowhere, signaling nowhere to go: "Lentils vegetate in the depths of
the fourth principal river of the world, the Ob, in Siberia, 3200 miles" (CB,
p. 3). Then another line explaining that what's being discussed is Quemoy
and Matsu, while (for the sake of a signally based joke) a sophomore at
the Famous Writers School in Westport, Connecticut takes notes, the narrator makes an observation about the young woman's breasts, Florence's
opening remarks on a leak in the upstairs bathroom are recalled, and
the paragraph itself concludes with an unsuccessful try at remembering
Herman Kahn's position on the disputed Chinese islands.

"Florence Green Is 81" continues in this manner for another thirteen
pages, expanding the nature of its opening paragraph into a method for
the entire story. Although it yields no kernel of meaning, the pattern is a
clear one, starting from the established scene, introducing a question, and
then leaving it unanswered as one apparently unrelated topic is followed
by another and then by a third and fourth, the only semblance of resolution coming when the second or third piece of randomness is returned
to briefly at the subsection's end. The initial disruption occupies the same
structural position it would in a conventional narrative, or even within
one of Barthelme's less complex stories; but instead of leading to a rhythm
of constriction and relaxation, surprise and reassurance, or even disorder

and reordering, there is no synthesis at all—just the replication of such useless information as a way of keeping all knowledge in the story completely disjunctive. In Barthelme's hands, it becomes the pure structure of disruption with no significant reliance on content at all, for the content referred to bears no purpose in terms of meaning.

What then is accomplished in the course of this story? Surely a deconditioning of the reader's expectations and a correlative opening to new experience within the text itself. To make that process easier, the author allows a certain incrementality to his junkstock of data. In the second paragraph the narrator berates Baskerville, the would-be famous writer, for bypassing the growth stage of worrying about life, and then drops in another piece of random information which at least comically touches the topic: "The smallest city in the United States with a population over 100,000 is Santa Ana, California, where 100,350 citizens nestle together in the Balboa blue Pacific evenings worrying about their lives" (CB, p. 4). From there, he addresses the reader directly, citing an article from the journal he edits that explains how patients in analysis fear they will bore their doctors, and how he intends to keep his readers from boredom by dazzling them with free association.

The narrator, then, shows himself to be much like the author Donald Barthelme, often taking time out from the story line to dazzle readers with novel twists of language much as Barthelme will do in the volume's simpler tales. "I am . . . the father of one abortion and four miscarriages" (CB, p. 5), he admits, and anticipates coming into a great deal of money that "would rain down like fallout in New Mexico" (CB, p. 8). His offhand remarks are patently disarming, not simply because of their surprising combinations but thanks to their range of elements; the story has begun with references to his table talk, fascination with the new young woman, and his editorship of a journal, but when the three come together again much later the results can be stunning, as in the narrator's exclamation that "Oh, there is nothing better than intelligent conversation except thrashing about in bed with a naked girl and Egmont Italic Light" (CB, p. 9).

Because of so many analogues between the narrator speaking to his psychiatrist and the author writing for the reader, "Florence Green Is 81" is ideally suited as an introduction to Barthelme's method, providing a course of instruction in reading this strange new style and even hinting why such style has become necessary. Citing a study published in his journal, Barthelme's character outlines a problem in psychiatric medicine suggesting the trials of fictive words in an age that has proclaimed the exhaustion of conventional technique and therefore the possible death of the novel: "*In such cases the patient sees the doctor as a highly sophisticated consumer of outré material, a connoisseur of exotic behavior. Therefore he tends to propose himself as more colorful, more eccentric (or more ill) than he really is; or he is witty, or he fantasticates*" (CB, p. 5). Are Barthelme's wild metaphors and surprising turns of plot an attempt to make himself appear interesting to a New Yorker readership lulled into anticipated predictability by three decades of John O'Hara stories? By the early 1960s, readers are certainly knowledgeable, the broad experience of high modernism having created as deep an understanding of short story art (from Anderson and Fitzgerald, through O'Hara to Flannery O'Connor, John Cheever, and the lately arrived Updike) as veteran psychiatrists would have learned from their patients. The comparison in terms of anxiety of reception is telling, and one appreciates that writing in the shadow of great modernists from Joyce to Faulkner might well be like speaking to an analyst in the hour following sessions with Dora and the wolf man. The plan Barthelme devises does fit the general description his character draws from the journal.

An element of self-critique is central to the story, just as years later *The Dead Father* will feature not just characters examining their own actions but a novelistic structure that pauses from time to time and questions the nature of its being. The purposes for such are manifold: entertaining but also instructing the reader at the same time the author experiments with his construction, readerly and writerly progress being made simultaneously. As for the story's proper action, it turns out to be nothing more than talk. Interesting talk to be sure, and an important part of life—"We value each other for our remarks" (CB, p. 15), the narrator confides. But like all action, this talk runs down, its entropy even more apparent as the decay of language itself. And so the final page of "Florence Green" peters out with the narrator's hopes for money slipping away, such subjects of Florence's conversation drifting off into fully undefined randomness, and his homeward-bound car turning in endless idiot circles on the street.

Equally true to itself, yet on terms that are extremely challenging, is the volume's other notably complex story, "The Viennese Opera Ball." Here, rather than bits of disjunctive information, the narrative presents several different stories simultaneously as the ball proceeds. Doctors describe and debate abortion; models and their fees are noted; arcane anthropological practices are detailed, and medical practices are recounted in a bizarre mix of language that mirrors the intersecting actions of the narrative, such as "The membranes were ruptured artificially and a Spanish windlass was applied. . . . Convalescence was satisfactory, and the patient was dismissed on the fourteenth postoperative day. Waiters with drinks circulated among the ball-goers" (CB, p. 87). As in "Florence Green," the result is a dizzying defamiliarization for the reader, opening gaps into which the author can drop displays of his amazing virtuosity, freed as the story now is from any need for consecutive logic and accumulative development. Conversations take the form of elaborate lists, a counting off of topics rather than any attempt to fashion them into dialogue. Included are lines typical of narrative development, such as "Far off at Barlow Ranger Station, as the dawn was breaking, Bart slept dreamlessly at last" (CB, p. 91), even though they have no bearing whatsoever on this story—but then again, how can such a deliberately random narrative have any bearing at all? Eventually the ball's action, which like "Florence Green" becomes a matter of dangling conversations, resolves itself as a page-long index of subjects, with page numbers running past 400. The story concludes with boiler plate data from appliances inserted as equal parts of the narrative while, as another introduction is made, "The Viennese Opera Ball continued" (CB, p. 94).

What has happened is that the Viennese opera ball has become "The Viennese Opera Ball," the subject of Barthelme's story becoming the story itself—a clever little operation on Samuel Beckett's prescription for postmodernism, that the literary work not be about something but be that something itself. In a similar way the author will craft his finest novel so that the hauling of the Dead Father becomes *The Dead Father* itself, its action in the referential world becoming identical with the action on the page. The opera ball continues, but our readerly attention dissipates even as the story's narrative action fizzles out in a state of entropy, much like the ending of "Florence Green Is 81" yet without the need for more external reference (the car circling endlessly on the drive home).

From the stories of *Come Back, Dr. Caligari* Barthelme will draw the technical resources needed to write his masterwork novel. Technical diversity is the volume's hallmark. Subsequent collections will ease off on the structural experimentation and develop themes instead, taking what in these early days would be a brilliant one liner (present in such stories as "The Joker's Greatest Triumph" and "Up, Aloft in the Air" for virtuoso effect) and drawing it out into a developed statement. This in itself is another step toward going the distance in a full-length novel. But it is important to consider the range of techniques available to Barthelme as early as 1964, a decade before writing The Dead Father, and all that those techniques contribute to our age's reformulation of the fictive act. From the light-hearted quotation of modernism come several factors: the anxiety of influence, of course, but also a comically comfortable attitude that acknowledging the great canons of knowledge shared by writer and reader also allows some jokes to be made, especially jokes that undo the modernist seriousness of purpose that would otherwise make such knowledge oppressive. Moreover, the very use of such materials undoes them; while Kafka finds his metamorphosis a threat, Barthelme makes it a pleasure, rewarding his protagonist with the same carnal delights he was only momentarily foolish to worry about. Without these techniques and the attitudes behind them, it is impossible to conceive of the Dead Father as he is handled in the novel of that name.

Equally instrumental in Barthelme's development toward The Dead Father is the reinforcement of story and structure, especially the tales of linguistic deconstruction that deconstruct themselves for us on the page. Initially simple demonstrations of this practice are built up into sustained narratives which systematically eliminate everything except system itself, reeducating readers even as the new form of story is accomplished in the process.

By the time Come Back, Dr. Caligari has been experienced, readers are prepared to appreciate a story's action in and for itself—an anticipation of how the simple act of cartage sustaining the narrative in The Dead Father will be sufficient to carry interest from beginning to end. At the same time, the author will use such a banally simple structure as an excuse for any number of apparent distractions and diversions. On the long march of his novel, any number of bizarre things happen, from a dialogue with feminism to an encounter with the influence of mothering. The genius of it all is that these intrusions never seem out of place, because the narrative's utter simplicity allows any number of modifications without having logic or development buckle under the weight. Consider how the dinner party for Florence Green and the grand opera ball are in themselves rudimentary affairs, whose only being consists in their progress in filling up the clock time of their existence. Yet within their obvious structures any number of things take place, quite startling by themselves but properly accommodated within the wide open limits of what can turn up during a party or a dance.

Above all, Barthelme is placing his action on the page, removing it from the shadowy world of ideas and representations and locating it in a realm the reader not only knows is artificial but which can be controlled by the act of reading. The language of these stories is something to be handled; in making it worthy of such attention, the author relocates the world of fiction into a concrete realm of its own. For such a revolutionary act, there is amazingly little iconoclasm, far less than in those other works of the 1960s that stretched metaphors to spectacular lengths (Richard Brautigan's *Trout Fishing in America*), smothered the page in a typographical riot of simultaneity (Steve Katz's *The Exagggerations of Peter Prince*, its physical playfulness beginning with the exaggerated spelling of the title's second word), or devised elaborate posings of the author writing his novel (Ronald Sukenick's *Up*), or the story writing itself (William H. Gass's *Willie Masters' Lonesome Wife*). Yet neither is it a matter of theme alone. *Dr. Caligari's* success lies in its effortless blend of subject and technique, providing evidence for a radically new style of fiction being presented to us almost fully formed. That something like *The Dead Father* would follow seems obvious. Yet five volumes of self-professed fragments come first, including most immediately a novel that declined to cohere or develop as such longer forms should—and, in the case of *The Dead Father*, could, without sacrificing any of the author's carefully postulated beliefs. Although there would be nothing redirectively new to be added—from these successive volumes the only specific innovation lies in the use of graphic collage to make certain linguistic points more clear—there is a certain deepening of interest and clarification of intent, all of which makes *The Dead Father* worth waiting for.

Chapter Two

Early Fiction as Theme

Through the mid-1960s and the 1970s the Barthelme bibliography reveals a strong and steady productivity, averaging ten stories per year placed in *The New Yorker* and occasionally such other major magazines as *Harper's* and the *Atlantic Monthly*. Following *Come Back, Dr. Caligari* and initiating this decade of the author's most sustained and concentrated work is *Snow White* (1967), a novel which irritated critics for not being much of a conventional novel at all, but rather an assemblage of fragments crafted much like the stories of Barthelme's first collection. Because it resists development in favor of such moment-by-moment technical display, it is best treated as one of the bracketing items in a study of *The Dead Father*, this central masterwork being understood in the company of both the novel that precedes it and the other novel, *Paradise* (1986), that follows.

Unspeakable Practices, Unnatural Acts (1968), however, occupies a key place in Barthelme's development. Here we see his techniques applied in a more conscious manner to the affairs of the day, affairs which did not exist in 1961 when stories such as "Me and Miss Mandible" were crafted. By 1968 American culture had transformed itself much as fiction had begun changing a few years earlier, and there was a consensus that the decade itself could be identified as something different. The 1950s, for example, had nothing quite like the figure of Robert Kennedy; nor did it have a fiction capable of describing him (as Philip Roth's despair at having to equal the likes of Richard Nixon recalls). By the late 1960s, however, time and technique intersect, and a story such as "Robert Kennedy Saved from Drowning" becomes not only possible but necessary.

If *Dr. Caligari* had been technically ahead of its time, *Snow White* and Un-

speakable Practices rest easy with Barthelme's already achieved technique and instead succeed in catching up with the decade's transformed topicality. Counter cultures and underground movements dominate both books, as do political instability, nontraditional attitudes and practices, and above all the celebration of an unconventional life style that soon becomes a convention in itself. Of the fifteen stories gathered for this second collection, only the previously unpublished "Alice" breaks new ground in terms of form. On the other hand, the thematic disruptions within this new set of stories are as dazzling as the purely technical aspects of Barthelme's earlier work. An Indian uprising paralyzes a modern city much like a guerrilla or terrorist attack; a massive balloon, nearly four miles in length, suddenly occupies New York's Fifth Avenue from Fourteenth Street to Central Park; a newspaper is composed by writers and editors concerned with the deconstructive rather than cognitive properties of language; military scientists forge new weapons made of similarly deconstructive words; novice writers face a competitive national exam; a police tactical squad assaults the ghetto with jazz music rather than tear gas; a pair of crewmen in a nuclear missile silo risk worldwide holocaust in a psychotic game of jacks; the actions of a new U.S. president are given a deconstructive reading; Robert Kennedy is captured in a series of freeze-frame fragments; and an increasingly recognizable couple, at times identified as Edward and Pia, take up housekeeping in a postmodern life whose rhythms fit the style of Barthelme rather than O'Hara, Updike, or Cheever. Only in the patently experimental "Alice" does form outstrip content, and even here the action is directed toward linguistically tilting a domestic scene by now familiar from the Edward and Pia stories.

Though the innovative emphasis has shifted from technique to theme and from form to content, there is a common thread to Barthelme's development in that both collections announce and in part achieve their disruption of the traditional by means of humor. The author's first inclination is to laugh at rather than flail angrily against the forms and themes of an earlier style, and his comedy is infectious. Just as the Kafkaesque probity of metamorphosis is undercut by relocating this action into the silly circumstance of a sixth grade classroom, so do the thematic disruptions of "The Indian Uprising" and "The Balloon" seem accommodative rather than alienating thanks to Barthelme's light-hearted attitude toward them.

Though his practices may be hostile toward tradition, their mood is not; these works prefer the pin prick of satire to the bludgeon of more serious critique, but even more significant is the feeling of receptivity that is encouraged by having the traditionally modernist themes and techniques regarded more as a matter of hilarity than of scorn. A vicious attack, by virtue of its deadly seriousness, increases an estimate of rival size and power; laughter deflates and disarms. Plus it is immensely more fun to chuckle at something than be driven to fits of anger.

Consider how the first paragraph of "The Indian Uprising" begins with a most familiar scene-setting line but then systematically transforms the occasion into one of domestic trivia, and how what would in traditional hands be a major disruption is here changed into a sleepy banality, which is itself an even greater shock:

> We defended the city as best we could. The arrows of the Comanches came in clouds. The war clubs of the Comanches clattered on the soft, yellow pavements. There were earthworks along the Boulevard Mark Clark and the hedges had been laced with sparkling wire. People were trying to understand. I spoke to Sylvia. "Do you think this is a good life?" The table held apples, books, long-playing records. She looked up. "No." (UP, p. 3)

Each sentence does its job in first establishing and then deflating traditional practice and attitude. When the arrows come "in clouds," the reader appreciates how the still conventional writer is using figurative language to characterize a scene that in the first line has been simply situational. When the war clubs resound off the "soft, yellow pavements," such figuration becomes complex, the mild contrast of "clouds" versus "arrows" now yielding to the harsher conflict of sound within the terms of "clattered" and "soft" ("yellow" being added to further soften the sense). To this point the approach is familiar, but when a street is identified as being in America yet named, in distinctly European fashion, for a recent military hero, a more radical disjunction is achieved—because, unlike the standard poetic practice of contrasting "clouds" and "arrows" or even "soft" and "clattered," the image of a street such as Third Avenue being renamed "Boulevard Mark Clark" (not even the more naturally sounding Mark Clark Boulevard) is a joke. As such, it unsettles the seriousness that even poetic practice has maintained, and clears the way for the hilarity of the paragraph's concluding lines, which in another context would not be funny at all. These sentences, introduced by the familiar Barthelme technique of dropping a line typical of existential uncertainty into an ill-fitting postmodernist context, reposition the reader's attitude for experiencing the story that follows, letting "The Indian Uprising" take place on a thoroughly different plane than the usual modernist tale of city dwellers under siege. The situation strikes the reader as acceptable, however, because it has been premised by a joke rather than a threat. A laughing audience is always more receptive than a defensive one.

With form thus opened up, the story's theme becomes accommodative of a broad new world of experience, the world being remade by the 1960s disruptions and transformations Barthelme is witnessing around him. When his people build barricades against the insurgents, the materials are not the usual paving stones but "window dummies, silk, thoughtfully planned job descriptions (including scales for the orderly progress of other colors), wine in demijohns, and robes" (UP, p. 5). In "The Balloon," when this gigantic and thoroughly unlikely object takes over a large part of their city, Barthelme's residents do not struggle against it but rather adapt and conform, accepting it as a new given and profiting immensely by accepting rather than resisting:

> There was a certain amount of initial argumentation about the "meaning" of the balloon; this subsided, because we have learned not to insist on meanings, and they are rarely even looked for now, except in cases involving the simplest, safest phenomena. It was agreed that since the meaning of the balloon could never be known absolutely, extended discussion was pointless, or at least less purposeful than the activities of those who, for example, hung green and blue paper lanterns from the warm grey underside, in certain streets, or seized the occasion to write messages on the surface, announcing their availability for the performance of unnatural acts, or the availability of acquaintances. (UP, p. 17)

What "The Balloon" accomplishes is a transfer of attention from the depths of meaning to the texture of surface, something the technical experiments of the stories in Come Back, Dr. Caligari brought into practice. Here the demonstration is made via a situational equivalent; the narrative itself is crafted in traditional form, the postmodern transformations couched quite easily within the stylistic developments of this last sentence that begins with a philosophical theorem and moves so smoothly into a physical description of colors, senses, and the most common yet consequential of inscribed messages. In Barthelme's case, and in the case of his readers, the technical facility has come first, a volume earlier. It is as if science has made a new discovery, the abilities of which are only realized after its technique has opened up new realms of experience. Once opened, the joy is in exploring them, and that is just what the stories in *Unspeakable Practices, Unnatural Acts* do.

The implications for writing an extended work such as *The Dead Father* are obvious. Technique has offered a great range of possibilities, and humor opens the way to their uncontested experience. The nature of the experience grows, writer and reader both learning how much is now at their disposal and how much exists to be explored. That theme offers as many possibilities as technique provides the chance for an extended narrative— not a new technical thrill beginning each page of a novel like *Snow White* (and therefore necessarily fragmenting the story line and interrupting the action), but rather a sustainable interest in a larger topic and grander sweep of activity.

Hints of such increasing range are evident throughout *Unspeakable Practices*. There are fewer stories generated by situational oddities and sustained by one-line jokes, while the collection boasts several major pieces that engage significant themes at some length. Chief among these more developed stories is "Robert Kennedy Saved from Drowning," a narrative whose overall succession within a set of fragments anticipates what Barthelme accomplishes in *The Dead Father*. Consisting of twenty-four individually titled sections, none longer than a page and usually just a paragraph or two in length, it combines the sharpness of separate identity with the integrity of a broader view. All of the sections, of course, refer to Kennedy, but their coherence is of a more functional nature, relating not just to the subject but to the writer's attempt at understanding him. Because he exists in real life (alive at the time of writing and first appearance in *New American Review*, and inscribed in the historical record when assassinated in the same season as the collection's publication) Kennedy presents a different type of challenge to both writer and reader. On the one hand, since an external reference already exists, the character need not be created out of nothing. On the other, Kennedy's existence can complicate matters, since the reader's fund of knowledge will supply details beyond Barthelme's control, with the chance of making an entirely different story. As author, Barthelme solves the latter problem by making Kennedy's aura of impenetrability one of the narrative's themes and also an index to its practice; for as bits and pieces about the man are assembled from sources here and there, the subject resists easy understanding and even an accumulative logical sense. Yet even as the subject of the narrative resists an integral summation, its structure justifies itself as a proof of Kennedy's ambiguity and conceptual aloofness, and by doing so reaches a logically developed conclusion about a subject that logic and development alone cannot grasp.

As befits the nature of this collection, a structural analogue is provided by the times. "Robert Kennedy Saved from Drowning" is compiled much like a television documentary, with clips from past and present assembled in collagelike fashion to form a picture puzzle of the man. Recalled by old school teachers, assessed by contemporary colleagues, and caught in candid moments with his family and his own thoughts, the subject of such a compilation is at once whole and fragmented. Moving further into technical structure, one sees that the story could be drawing on a formal state even anterior to a finished documentary, such as a reporter's still unorganized notes or the outtakes and unedited wildtrack from a film crew's stock of material. Both the TV documentary and the featured use of outtakes are prominent media in the 1960s, just as is the cinema vérité / behind-the-scenes nature of their use; part of the age's aesthetic is that what litters the cutting room floor may be more truthful and insightful than the final product of editing.

There is also a strong element of humor to this story, both in theme and overall technical accomplishment. Robert Kennedy's opacity leads to his every action being wondered at and revered like an icon—laughing matter when those actions are in fact quite trivial. And although the story is patterned as a quest for knowledge, it soon becomes an antiepistemology, for it starts with a well-known character and ends knowing virtually nothing—or at least less than the reader did before. When the man speaks, it is in multisyllabic generalities, words which are terms related to function rather than content. When his quotes are overheard, they are worse than enigmatic, for his comments on a painter in the style of Mondrian are banally reductive while his observations on the exotic are tediously mundane. Photo opportunities, as with a family gathering, have the awkward feel of a failed snapshot; even a master portraitist such as Karsh of Ottawa, famous for his definitive posings of Churchill and Hemingway, complains how hard it is to get the right shot. The clearest insight is one Kennedy cites himself, Georges Poulet's analysis of "the Marivaudian being" as a "pastless futureless man, born anew at every instant," these instances organizing themselves into a line which is less important than the instant (UP, p. 46). Thus there is no sense of history, no appreciation of what has gone before: just the instant of surprise.

As a formulation of literary structure, this explanation anticipates the description of the typical Tralfamadorian novel in Kurt Vonnegut's *Slaughterhouse-Five* (1969), where there are no beginnings, middles, or ends, but just the depth of many marvelous moments seen all at one time. Vonnegut's own novel follows this aesthetic not just by skipping around in time and space from one fragment of experience to another (causing them to be related on terms other than chronological or juxtapositional order), but by frustrating the reader's understandable attempt to make the succeeding pages accumulate in meaning, thereby holding off such judgment until the book's end, where its separate parts can be appreciated in their totality. Barthelme's Kennedy story does much the same, never coming into personal contact with the man until the very last segment, when a drowning Kennedy is saved by the narrator, here (in the moment of emergency) identifying himself for the first time as "I." When the sum of Kennedy's response is a simple "Thank you"—far less than said to a waiter several fragments earlier when making selections from the menu—the effect of twenty-three previous takes suddenly becomes cumulative, all in one overwhelming blow. As a readerly experience, it compares to the ending of *The Dead Father*, when after twenty-three short and often digressively fragmentary chapters on the way to the dead father's burial (one of them framing a twenty-three-part manual on the subject), the figure is finally bulldozed into his grave.

Robert Kennedy's resistance to summation, then, is the story's sum meaning, a conclusion less satisfying in itself than as a process the reader can enjoy being taken through. One common feature to the stories in *Unspeakable Practices, Unnatural Acts* is their performative exuberance. Especially effective are the little motifs the reader can cue on to, such as the regular habit of naming the urban demography of "The Indian Uprising"—not just the Boulevard Mark Clark, but Rue Chester Nimitz, George C. Marshall Allée, Patton Place, and Skinny Wainwright Square. Thanks to their repetition in form, the reader is taken up in the story's generative process, and before long can enjoy anticipating what other American military leader's name will be affixed to a street sign and what other bizarre materials will go into the making of barricades. Like pieces in a jigsaw puzzle, the fragmented shapes of Robert Kennedy take on a character all their own, as readers begin searching not for an eye, a nose, or a piece of blue sky but rather a funny little section twisted this way or that. It is the manner in which *The Dead Father* coheres, a matter of formal relation and structural system as much as theme, although theme has certainly come first.

The technical aspects of *Unspeakable Practices, Unnatural Acts* are, as in *The Dead Father*, usually announced as themes, but themes that demonstrate their technique with their very presence. A minor character in "The Indian Uprising" seems there principally to announce her preference for a certain kind of discourse, the litany, which confines itself to what can safely be said. The narrator himself prefers more elaborate "strings of language," but admits that even a rudimentary form like the litany serves just as well "to bind the world together into a rushing, ribald whole" (UP, p. 11), as a perusal of any of the lists Barthelme has been favoring since his first stories will show. Where no order is prescribed, the reader's eye invents one, for such is the systematizing favored by words once placed in the context of language; syntax, like the ecological system of nature, abhors a vacuum. But to remain alive, systems demand disruption and remodification. This happens in "The Balloon," when the huge amorphous structure imposes itself upon the grid system of New York's streets. In linguistic terms, the balloon seems purposeless. "Had we painted, in great letters, 'LABORATORY TESTS PROVE' or '18% MORE EFFECTIVE' on the sides of the balloon," the narrator realizes, "this difficulty would have been circumvented" (UP, p. 18). But the story's theme is how the citizens learn to revel in this new, apparently disorderly sense of order, locating themselves in reference to its new geographic definitions and taking joy in its relative lack of limits, all of which offers the possibility of change in a world to which such an idea had been anathema.

The life-giving force of such disruption—of life as an alternative to systematically predicated death—is discussed in "This Newspaper Here," the story of an old man who wards off the evitable by shifting modes, just as the news content of the paper he reads occasionally yields to paragraphs of compositional play, lines of (!) (!) (!) (!) (!) (!) (!) and * * * * * * * alternating with ? / ? / ? / ? / ? / and o: o: o: o: o: o: o: to form paragraphs aesthetically attractive yet linguistically meaningless. The choice is a wise one, when advancing age makes one more vulnerable to the inexorable march of history and eligible for obituaries the paper usually prints. For the same reason the man's personal library consists of telephone books, directories to the "names from Greater Memphis Utica Key West Toledo Santa Barbara St. Paul Juneau Missoula Tacoma and every which where" (UP, p. 29), a pleasurable riot of associations unfettered by conclusive meaning (yet with an abundance of unthreatening meanings just the same). In a similar way dead language itself can be rejuvenated, clichés turned back into vibrant metaphors by shaking up the terms of tenor and vehicle. Richard Brautigan was a master of this technique in *Trout Fishing in America* and *In Watermelon Sugar*, but in his story "Report" Barthelme fixes the references to a solid topic, an assessment by military scientists and engineers of the new weapons they are developing. The cold war climate of the 1950s had talked such considerations to death, and now in 1968 the country's antiwar sentiment was making them distasteful, but the author transforms both limitations by having his experts boast that "We have rots, blights, and rusts capable of attacking [the enemy's] alphabet" (UP, p. 55), "the deadly testicle-destroying telegram," and "a secret word that, if pronounced, produces multiple fractures in all living things in an area the size of four football fields" (UP, p. 56). In terms of transforming the leaden lack of imagination in jargon, the prize winner is their advance in computer technology, at this time still a mystifying pseudoscience; therefore it is most interesting to consider the possibilities of "realtime online computer-controlled wish evaporation," something crucial in "meeting the rising expectations of the world's peoples, which are as you know rising entirely too fast" (UP, p. 54).

Occasions such as these generate stories from their stock of typical language. Jazz musicians have their own argot and manners, together with an informing legend (jazz coming up the river from New Orleans and Memphis to Chicago, the big bands sweeping dancers off their feet, the tortured genius of Charlie Parker, the icy aloofness of Miles Davis, and so forth); from this wealth of material Barthelme has little trouble putting together "The Police Band," a simple exercise in transposing all this ambience from the nightclub stage to the police department's tac squad truck. "The Commissioner (the old Commissioner, not the one they have now) brought us up the river from Detroit" (UP, p. 73), we learn from the narrator, who adds that their duties were simple: to wail. Having a tactically trained jazz combo on hand, tense situations could be cooled down, urban volatility smothered in the changes to "Entropy" and angry crowds defused by one chorus of "Perdido." Like an Ernst collage, the materials from two distinct worlds face off in one action, the musicians streaming from the armored van with instruments at port arms and quickly taking up positions (a line of saxes supported by trumpets, with trombones interjecting on the upbeats) to change the crowd's ugly mood with the rapture of an Ellington number: "Our emotion stronger than their emotion. A triumph of art over good sense" (UP, p. 75). The crowd is believable because it acts, or at least has started to act, like a crowd; the police are doing their police-like business, dispersing the troublemakers; but the cops are also fully in character as jazz musicians, "Emptying spit valves, giving the horns that little shake. Or coming in at letter E with some sly emotion from another life" (UP, p. 74). As in the best of Barthelme's collages, the effect is linguistic as well as topical, as the jargon in the closing phrase slides easily from the mundane reference to the score to a jazz critic's typical appraisal of what's being played.

Despite such brightly presented satire, which will remain in Barthelme's repertoire to enliven the action of *The Dead Father* and even *Paradise* two decades later, there is a decided note of impending exhaustion to the stories of *Unspeakable Practices, Unnatural Acts*—most obviously a sense that there will come a point of diminishing returns in the constant attempt to devise catchy new themes. As one last use of the principally thematic, Barthelme presents "The Dolt," detailing the fate of a character named Edgar as he prepares to take the National Writers' Examination. In crafting stories, Edgar is brilliant at endings but has a bit more trouble with middles, the conclusions often coming first and demanding narrative justification.

His writer's workshop is then rudely interrupted by his teenage son, in response to whom Edgar finds himself equally helpless in coming up with words. In a rare shift of person, Barthelme slips from a third-person omniscient to a confessional "I," sympathizing with the man's inability to think of anything to say. "I myself have these problems," the newly present narrator admits, taking his place as the maker of this otherwise inconsequential story. "Endings are elusive, middles are nowhere to be found, but worst of all is to begin, to begin, to begin" (UP, p. 69).

As if to solve his problem, Barthelme moves on to another style of story rounding out this collection, going from his dazzling virtuosity on the canvas's flat surface to a new hard edge of narrative. Here are found the Edward and Pia stories, cautious little narratives that reduce themselves to a phenomenology of action no more spectacular than a typical work by Sarraute or Robbe-Grillet. In the company of the more appealing themes of the volume's earlier tales, "Edward and Pia" and "A Few Moments of Sleeping and Waking" seem just the style of work Barthelme had faulted in his essay from the second number of *Location* (Summer 1964), "After Joyce":

> The new French novelists, Butor, Sarraute, Robbe-Grillet, Claude Simon, Philippe Sollers, have . . . succeeded in making objects of their books without reaping any of the strategic benefits of the maneuver— a triumph of misplaced intelligence. Their work seems leaden, self-conscious in the wrong way. Painfully slow-paced, with no leaps of the imagination, concentrating on the minutiae of consciousness, these novels scrupulously, in deadly earnest, parse out what can safely be said. In an effort to avoid psychologism and unwarranted assumptions they arrive at inconsequence, carrying on that traditional French war against the bourgeois which ends by flattering him: what a monster! (*Location* #2, p. 16)

Although his own motives are different, occasioned by the fear of running out of bright new themes rather than worrying about unjustified personalist assumptions, Barthelme nevertheless finds himself with the same consequent emphasis on the materiality of life. Edward and Pia are the ideal couple to place in a contemporary furnished room, the narrative checking off their habits and possessions like so many items in a designer catalog. Because in the first story Edward counts his money and worries about his constantly dwindling resources, everything he encounters is not only named but priced. In the second the couple catalogs their meetings according to various books of dream interpretation, though the analyses are never explored, just identified. The author's way out of this predicament is found in "Alice," a Beckettian throwback which at least gets him off the nouveau roman track by alternating paragraphs of swirling, Joycean language such as "twirling around on my piano stool my head begins to swim my head begins to swim twirling around on my piano stool twirling around on my piano stool a dizzy spell eventuates twirling around on my piano stool I feel dizzy twirling around on my piano stool" (UP, p. 119) with similar sized passages recounting a string of intricately proposed fornications. The achievement reminds one of Beckett's hero systematizing the stones he'll suck on various days of the week—a nice transposition of the Joycean modern into Beckett's postmodern and a way of avoiding the dead end of the nouveau romanciers, but no real development in Barthelme's own art. At best it provides a landscape usable in *The Dead Father*; but as a short form, it shares little with Barthelme's methods of this period, other than showing how quiet his fiction becomes when they are removed.

Yet Barthelme is not about to say goodbye to the funny little touches he sees in language all about us. Those touches may not be capable of supporting extended themes—trying to make them do so accounts for some of his admitted exhaustion—but when the silliness of certain words can be traced to the system that produces them, the results are still stimulating. Religion and politics are two favorite subjects the author prefers to treat in terms of systematics rather than content; indeed, his opinion might well be that they are all system and no content at all, given the way his characters handle them. Consider the paragraph in "A Picture History of the War" when the protagonist goes to confession:

> Kellerman falls to his knees in front of the bench. "Bless me, Father, for I have sinned. I committed endoarchy two times, melanicity four times, encropatomy seven times, and preprocipity with igneous intent, pretolemicity, and overt cranialism once each." (UP, p. 133)

The Latinate terms, proper to a medical dictionary, recall that Catholicism is the other major user of this language; plus their mood of doctrinaire theology suggests both the technicality and bureaucracy of sin. The odd words are not only listed but are modified in kind ("with igneous intent"); and just when the reader agrees that these undecipherable words suggest that church practice is smothering free thought with intellectual hocus-pocus, Barthelme drops in a more direct derivation, "overt cranialism," for a deft thematic touch. But the joke isn't over yet, for the priest must also speak in turn. His words are so much simpler, but in a way that regenerates the entire system: "Within how long a period?" Politics are an even easier target, particularly in the age of 1960s' disaffection with the mainstream and the alienation of leadership from the culture. In "The President," Barthelme's narrator complains that he cannot tell what the man is thinking or remember what he has said just moments before; newspapers are no more helpful, reporting merely that he "touched on a number of matters in the realm of . . ." (UP, p. 149).

Religion and politics come from the culture, allowing Barthelme to make direct borrowings. Gigantic balloons and an attack on postmodern New York by a tribe of Comanches do not, and even though the author faces them off against his familiar life it takes a great deal of energy to create such imaginative situations—energy that, in volumes collecting fourteen or fifteen short stories, is bound to be exhausting for both author and audience. The piece that concludes *Unspeakable Practices, Unnatural Acts*, a fondly titled story asking "See the Moon?", finds the narrator begging his listener not to go, that "the greased-pig chase and balloon launchings come next" (UP, p. 161), an entreating of the reader as much as of the character to whom it is addressed. This story is built on the most obvious autobiographical references in Barthelme's canon, including his duties at the newly made University of Houston writing "poppycock for the president" (UP, p. 156) and his military service in Korea. Especially revealing are his comments on the art world he came to know as a museum director in Houston and an art journal editor in New York during the heyday of Action Painting, Pop, Op, Conceptual, Minimal, and Hard Edge: "I wanted to be a painter. They get away with murder in my view." Yet it is a writer that his narrator is sentenced to be, prompting the statement that critics would take as the most autobiographical of all: "Fragments are the only form I trust" (UP, p. 157).

Why art as an ideal, and why fragments as a literary practice? The an-swers to each and particularly the connection between the two tell much about Donald Barthelme's aesthetic, not just in his early stories but in the talents and ideas that make his later novel possible. The style of painting Barthelme inherited as a young man was abstract expressionism, the type of work done by Jackson Pollock, Willem de Kooning, Franz Kline and others in which (according to Barthelme's boss at *Location*, Harold Rosen-berg) the canvas was less of a surface upon which to represent than an arena in which to act. As Beckett had postulated for postmodernism, the work would not be about something, but be that something itself. For painting, an abstract expressionist's tactic was simply to let the paint be its own subject and its action on the canvas its own narrative; Barthelme, as a museum director and sometime critic, could well appreciate how Pollock's "Blue Poles" could be watched as a movie with no need for won-dering where were the poles and why were they blue. But what of fiction? Even the author's most abstract and performative story, "Alice," is made out of words; and words, unlike daubs of paint, refer to things or ideas outside of themselves, and so by nature direct their readers to a quest the author cannot prevent or control.

Barthelme's stories, particularly those in his next collection, *City Life* (1970), show evidence of responding to this challenge that *Unspeakable Prac-tices, Unnatural Acts* has tried to deal with on the exhausting level of theme. But on a critical level the author has these goals in mind from the start. *Location*, the managing editor's job which brought him from Houston to New York, had begun with manifestolike statements by its founders, Harold Rosenberg and Thomas B. Hess, and continued in its second (and unfortunately last) issue with Barthelme's "After Joyce," further advancing what the journal proposed as an aesthetic for its time. This second number also included a Barthelme story, "For I'm the Boy," inviting the readers' judgments of theory and practice, issue and response.

Reading Barthelme's essay in the context of what we now recognize as his innovative fiction, it becomes clear that even though he discusses modernist writers, he is outlining an ideal not always achieved in their work and certainly not granted by their readers. As in the case of Beckett appreciating the art-object status of *Finnegans Wake*, it would take a postmodern assessment to draw out these features, one that Barthelme makes near the beginning of "After Joyce":

> Satisfied with neither the existing world nor the existing literature, Joyce and Stein modify the world by adding to its store of objects the literary object—which is then encountered in the same way as other objects in the world. The question becomes: what is the nature of the new object? Here one can see an immediate result of the shift. Interrogating older works, the question is: what do they say about the world and being in the world? But the literary object is itself "world" and the theoretical advantage is that in asking it questions you are asking questions of the world directly. This sounds like a species of ventriloquism—the writer throwing his voice. But it is, rather, a stunning strategic gain for the writer. He has in fact removed himself from the work, just as Joyce instructed him to do. The reader is not listening to an authoritative account of the world delivered by an expert (Faulkner on Mississippi, Hemingway on the corrida) but bumping into something that is *there*, like a rock or a refrigerator. (Location #2, p. 13)

When viewers so often ask of modern painting *what is it?* they are admitting that they themselves are encountering something strange and new; in similar manner, "the reader reconstitutes the work by his active participation, by approaching the object, tapping it, shaking it, holding it to his ear to hear the roaring within" (p. 14).

Barthelme, then, is not the first fiction writer to envy the advantage of painting and emulate its effect on an audience. But as in "Me and Miss Mandible," he understands how readers anxious for grounding in the real world, be it by myth or psychology, can take what the modernists offer and receive it as referential material. Certain techniques can short-circuit that reception, such as turning the readers' appreciation of a metamorphosis into a joke (so that the pleasure of its operations can be felt) or breaking up the ongoing narrative flow into fragments, the only forms trustworthy enough to allow an appreciation of themselves rather than something represented. The implications for an extended work like *The Dead Father* are clear: can a narrative about the parental order's unyielding need to dominate and the filial set's desire to move on be anything other than a Freudian report? Or, more personally, can the artistic urge to deal with these materials produce anything beyond psychology, sociology, or myth? And in terms of Barthelme's own development, with a second collection of short stories completed and a third under way, can the successful struggle against such outdated literary theories be fueled by anything except an ultimately exhausting series of clever techniques and dazzlingly instructive themes? As the author moves quickly to solidify his reputation in the genre, with three short story collections published inside five years, the ability to present fiction as its own object matures as one of his most secure talents.

Chapter Three

Toward Sustained Narrative

Systems

_____

City Life (1970), *Sadness* (1972), and *Guilty Pleasures* (1974) are the collections that seal Barthelme's reputation not only as a short story master
but as the direction-setting writer of his age. In them he achieves a
balance between the pyrotechnic surprises of *Come Back, Dr. Caligari* and the
culturally thematic lessons of *Unspeakable Practices, Unnatural Acts*, with one
new technique—the collage story—thrown in for fresh spice. They are
especially helpful in fashioning an interpretation of his work, for within
them can be seen virtually everything promised by his earliest stories and
most of the qualities highlighted by going the distance in *The Dead Father*.
Little of what made the author so appealing in the early 1960s is lost: the
stories can still be riotously funny, and pretensions of literature, politics,
religion, and social practice remain as vulnerable as ever to his satiric barbs.
But there is a new strength evident in how his narratives are sustained, not
by technique or theme alone, as before, but with an integral combination
of the two.

Such integration is evident from the start, as "Views of My Father
Weeping" leads off *City Life* with a narrative style that puts Barthelme
straight on the road to *The Dead Father*. If *Unspeakable Practices* had ended with
the thought that fragments were the only form to trust, then "Views of My
Father Weeping" is an eminently trustworthy story. Like "Robert Kennedy
Saved from Drowning," it consists of short little segmented vignettes, now
half again as many (thirty-six) in the same number of pages. But unlike
the antiepistemological business of the Kennedy story, this new piece approaches the acquisition of knowledge as a reasonable task, not one to be
frustrated by the essential unknowability of the subject. Here the situation

is a simple one: a narrator trying to trace the details of his father's death (in which he fails) and by doing so achieve an understanding of what his father was to him and what his loss entails (in which the narrator succeeds). The story's success on these latter terms signals Barthelme's developing interest in process rather than effect, and alerts readers to a sustaining of interest in how the narrative is worked out as opposed to being jiggled and jostled by individual techniques.

"An aristocrat was riding down the street in his carriage. He ran over my father" (CL, p. 3). With these introductory lines that constitute the entire first section of his story the author avoids the anxieties of devising interesting plots (for a world bored by them), justifying his endings by elaborate explanations (to readers skeptical of the very best ones), and above all wondering (in the words of "The Dolt") how "to begin, to begin, to begin" (UP, p. 69). All are avoided because this narrative has begun with what in conventional terms would be an ending. If the worry toward the end of his previous collection had been of exhaustion, this new volume begins at the other side of that possibility: with what happens to the literary work when its author has already concluded that not just the traditional ways of telling stories are exhausted but that the writer's energy for counteracting such exhaustion are themselves depleted. "Views of My Father Weeping" thus moves a step beyond the innovation already undertaken by John Barth, who'd argued that the entropic state of contemporary literary arts demanded a recourse to parody, satire, and inspired imitation. Barth's strategy leads to another possibility, it is true; but as an imitation of an imitation of an action, it remains bound to the aesthetic that's supposed to be worn out. By beginning with the end, as it were, Barthelme puts such problems behind him and starts with a fresh slate in a realm of writerly action never yet inscribed.

As an epistemology, his story has to justify its existence by asking the right questions. Not ones that lead back to the beginning (a conventional story's end), such as "trying to think of the reason why my father died." Memory solves that one immediately: "he was run over by a carriage" (CL, p. 3). This internal dialogue with the narrator's self forms the second section of "Views of My Father Weeping," and shows the direction in which the story cannot go if it wishes to be successful. Soon come other options:

asking his mother (who says everything happens for the best, a typical characterization that has made the maternal another dead end among post-modern possibilities), questioning his own perception (wondering if the father in his visions is someone else), and realizing how even eyewitness accounts are never fully reliable.

What the narrator returns to are his memories, especially those that resist verification by testing. They are of the type that defy rationalization anyway: the father sitting at the center of his bed and weeping, tossing a ball of yarn into the air (where it hangs in a freeze frame of remembrance), and all the time lingering like a phantom, just out of reach. The ungraspable nature of these flashbacks is what distinguishes the story from history (Ronald Sukenick's caution) and allows the narrator an open field for narrating (in a world whose rational possibilities have foreclosed any chances for statement). Convention still provides a structure: following a trail of clues to find the killer, just as The Dead Father uses the serial device of hauling the subject across a landscape from which will emerge episodic adventures. But on that structure are hung entirely different sorts of narrative occasions—ones that modally deepen the character's and the readers' sense not just of who this father was but how his loss affects the son. It is surely no accident that the topicality of story and novel are the same, for Barthelme is finding a subject that his special talents and unique ideals for narrative can sustain.

Having begun with a story that shows how much farther the author can extend his narrative, City Life continues with a series of more specific exercises based on new techniques for building fiction. In "Sentence," the most basic of these shorter works, Barthelme sets himself the challenge of writing an entire story, well over two thousand words, consisting of just one sentence. It begins in mid-phrase, "Or a long sentence moving at a certain pace down the page aiming for the bottom—if not the bottom of this page then of some other page—where it can rest, or stop for a moment to think about the questions raised by its own (temporary) existence, which ends when the page is turned, or the sentence falls out of the mind that holds it (temporarily)" (CL, p. 107), and proceeds through several pages of what can happen not just to the sentence but to the reader reading it (a world of possibilities, yet generated by the sentence's existence) until concluding with a reminder that "the sentence itself is a man-made object, not the one we wanted of course, but still a construction of man, a structure to be treasured for all its weakness, as opposed to the strength of stones" (CL, p. 114).

Other stories seek out situations in which sentences stand by themselves, as in lines of conversation or advancements of the action, and devise ways of making them apparent, the better to be appreciated as the fabricated objects "Sentence" describes. "City Life" uses the European convention of marking off dialogue not with quotations but with an initial dash (a technique Barthelme likes so much that he centers several stories upon it in *Great Days*, his collection published in 1976). Though most of the exchanges are quick-paced and to the immediate point, their obviousness on the page lets the author ridicule how awkward the conventions of exposition by dialogue can be:

—Well, Ramona, I am glad we came to the city. In spite of everything.
—Yes, Elsa, it has turned out well for you. You are Mrs. Jacques Tope now. And soon there will be a little one.
—Not so soon. Not for eight months. I am sorry, though, about one thing. I hate to give up Law School.
—Don't be sorry. The Law needs knowledgeable civilians as well as practitioners. Your training will not be wasted.
—That's dear of you. Well, goodbye. (CL, p. 157)

In "The Glass Mountain," every sentence is numbered and set separately on the page; the narrator's progress up the side of a skyscraper is thus noted in stages, but his references to other parts of the action, such as his friends' calls of "encouragement" (which are actually insults and animadversions), thereby stand out as self-evident sentences. "Kierkegaard Unfair to Schlegel" lets narrative paragraphs alternate with sets of questions and answers, emphasizing the story's mode of inquiry. "The Explanation" is all Q's and A's, including a query as to whether the respondent is bored with the form; he is, but admits it allows "many valuable omissions: what kind of day it is, what I'm wearing, what I'm thinking. That's a very considerable advantage, I would say" (CL, p. 73).

These highlightings of the sentence let Barthelme vary the pace, break up his page, and at the same time allow comments on the advantages such disruptions of tradition achieve. But because a line of dialogue—whether punctuated with a dash, numbered, or set out as questions and answers—is a naturally existing form within the syntax of our language, he is able to feature it without destroying the one basic convention he still needs in order to be a writer rather than a painter or collagist: that of using words themselves.

In terms of their referentiality, then, the distinction for words would be not just the fact that they are used in fiction, but how they are used. The self-interrogation of a sentence working its way down the page does not allow it to be read the same way as a sentence in a realistic novel, let alone a sentence in a newspaper, biography, or historical account. Numbering sentences distinguishes them as units while still letting the narrative proceed, albeit in a way that invites the reader to see how that progress is achieved by syntactic components rather than by an effortless drift of imagination (drawing his analogy from linguists' use of morphemes and phonemes to distinguish minimal units of meaning, Roland Barthes divides the story of Balzac's *Sarrasine* into lexemes, units of narrative meaning whose structure can then be analyzed in Barthes' *S/Z*). The question and answer format is an even more dramatic display of how self-apparent units, and not just words, carry forth narrative; by the time of *Great Days*, the author will be so adept with this method that he can use the playful pleasure of a knock-knock joke for one of his most telling emotional effects.

Yet a thematization of technique alone would not be carrying Barthelme beyond the innovative status of *Come Back, Dr. Caligari*, and might well invite the risks of exhaustion that characterize *Unspeakable Practices, Unnatural Acts*. Therefore it is important to consider how the author's careful and rewarding attention to the sentence as the key building unit of his trade (akin to the painter's use of gesture with paint and the composer's arrangement of notes for melody) paves the way for a more abstract use of language in *City Life*'s more unusual stories.

The pieces collected here that provide the next set of challenges are "The Falling Dog," "Paraguay," and "Bone Bubbles." In the first, Barthelme starts with a clear but surprising event, as a large dog falls on the narrator from a window far overhead. Facing this unexplained circumstance, he feels compelled to justify it, and in so doing fashions a conventional story (including a mysterious beautiful woman, seductive intrigue and the possibilities of romance, a threat from another man, etc.). But as this framed narrative, like a vexing dream, refuses to take a pleasing or rewarding shape, the speaker shifts gears and starts breaking down the materials of his tale into Barthesean lexemes, set on the page as interrogations and inventories:

> I looked at the dog. He looked at me.
>
> who else has done dogs?
> Baskin, Bacon, Landseer, Hogarth,
> Hals
>
> with leashes trailing as they fall
>
> with dog impedimenta following:
> bowl, bone, collar, license, Gro-pup (CL, p. 33)

The narrator, now identified as a Welsh sculptor (just as the dog is called an Irish setter), inserts any number of things into the text, including a letter from his German dealer, a checklist of doggish metaphors, and other canine images that might be crafted into art. Without having to wonder what the falling dog means, the artist is freed from the need to explain (that is, to write a conventional story) and can instead hurry into his studio to produce the kind of art Barthelme's earlier narrator in "See the Moon?" so envied.

In "Paraguay" the author takes another step toward achieving just such work in language without having to devise a theme about it. As Roland Barthes would do just a few years later in *Roland Barthes par Roland Barthes* (1975), Barthelme distracts the inclination to form narratives by segmenting his story with terms for discussion: *temperature, error, rationalization, skin, terror,* and the like. Each word is then handled for a paragraph, handled in a way that allows both writer and reader to appreciate the texture of its being (both in physical properties and in associations). At its simplest, the technique allows ideas to be explored for their material effect, as in this treatment of the term *silence*:

> In the larger stores silence (damping materials) is sold in paper sacks like cement. Similarly, the softening of language usually lamented as a

falling off from former practice is in fact a clear response to the prolif-
eration of surfaces and stimuli. Imprecise sentences lessen the strain
of close tolerances. Silence is also available in the form of white noise.
(CL, p. 24)

Such conceptual enchantment is possible thanks to the poetic qualities of
language (the soft s sounds) but also because the story's format invites such
intriguing information, structured as it is (detailing the features of a relatively unfamiliar country). Within this framework, there is room for almost
any type of language, from lumberyard jargon in the midst of this same
paragraph—"Wood is becoming rare. They are now paying for yellow pine
what was formerly paid for rosewood"—to the grab bag of terminology
in the sentence that concludes it: "Electrolytic jelly exhibiting a capture
ratio far in excess of standard is used to fix the animals in place" (CL, p. 25),
which mixes language from the worlds of medicine, sound recording, and
taxidermy.

Most radical of the three is "Bone Bubbles," which like the previously
unpublished stories from Barthelme's first two collections takes the most
technically extreme practice from the volume and pushes it much further—further, in fact, than the author wants to go in terms of canonical
style. It is the self-indulgence taken by an adventurous writer working so
steadily to advance fiction within the confines of a conservative magazine
like The New Yorker and thereby gives the reader a hint of all the things
Barthelme could do if he threw tradition completely to the winds. As an
exercise in almost pure abstraction, it accomplishes what William Burroughs achieves in his cut-up fictions, an emphatic discarding of ideas so
that language will have to stand by itself. Yet as Barthelme admits when discussing Burroughs's cut-ups in the "After Joyce" essay, the method is essentially destructive: facing off disembodied words and unrelated phrases so
that their conceptual meanings are not so much defused (or diffused) as
destroyed in head-on collisions. "He has approximated what might be
heard tuning across the broadcast band of a radio built to receive all the
asylums of the world," Barthelme quips, and critiques Burroughs's tactic by borrowing the same style of jargon as used in "Paraguay": "A high
noise-to-signal ratio, randomness, and shouts of pain mingle to produce
an unbearable tension" (Location #2, p. 15).

Such aggression is only one way of circumventing reference. The other is play, and in "After Joyce" Barthelme selects his own favorite player: Samuel Beckett. Reductionary like a painter in that he throws ideas away in a quest to have mere combinations of material suggest meaning, Beckett provides a happier model for an author who has found his conservative readers more likely to react with favor to joking than intimidation. There is a Beckettian flavor to much of Barthelme's early fiction, especially the parties that drift along like people waiting for Godot and the conversations that seem generated more by mathematical permutations than situational stimuli and consequential logic.

When Barthelme decides to open up the gates to play, however, he reaches back to one of the more enjoyable phases of his career: the years spent as a managing editor (of *Forum* and then *Location*), not only searching out, gathering, and selecting items to print but cutting and pasting them together to form a pleasing layout. Parts of "Kierkegaard Unfair to Schlegel" and "The Explanation," first published in 1968, anticipate what he will do in the two succeeding years with "At the Tolstoy Museum" and "Brain Damage" by collaging in nonverbal elements to break up his words yet still advance the narrative. In the Kierkegaard story, the interpolation is of a single blackened square filling half of one page and serving to interrupt the narrator's confession, underscoring the irony of his making a climactic statement and then retracting it. (Unfortunately, the compromised layout of subsequent paperback editions moves this block to a more random position amid the subsequent sentences.) "The Explanation" features four such blocks more functionally (although the paperback resetting is now worse than random, for it disrupts their illustrative purpose), providing an object the interrogator and person being interrogated can discuss and figuring as a material presence in their narrative, positioned as it is after such comments as "Look at it" and ". . . show you a picture of my daughter" (CL, pp. 75, 79).

The blank box inserted in the text is actually a common journalistic device used at the stage of laying out a page when the story is already typeset but the accompanying photographs are not yet available (or needed in their illustrative form for the design). In these two stories, it allows Barthelme to break up his text and signal the presence of an illustration without having to provide the actual picture. The reader thus knows an object is being handled but need not be distracted by its own referentiality, letting the writer convey the notion of a *picture* of a house without unleashing the conceptuality involved in a picture of a *house*. It is a technique much more playful than aggressive, and by virtue of its familiarity as a layout practice focuses attention on the page. Yet these stories do offer the chance to use real pictures, and within the year Barthelme begins doing just that.

"At the Tolstoy Museum" begins with a full-page engraving of the supposed museum's subject, the Count himself in all his mystic glory. Turning the page reveals how Barthelme is undertaking a narrative with this piece of graphics, for an initial glance suggests that the same picture is being repeated. But one small element has been added: a one-and-a-quarter-inch cutout of a tiny Napoleon in profile, staring up from the lower left margin to contemplate Tolstoy's awesome visage (all the more imposing as it stands five inches tall, from crown to beard, up and down the page).

Finally on page three the text begins, recounting a visit to this museum that holds and displays thirty thousand pictures of the great man. In his own third paragraph, the narrator creates a verbal museum by counting off some random but curious facts:

> Tolstoy means "fat" in Russian. His grandfather sent his linen to Holland to be washed. His mother *did not know* any bad words. As a youth he shaved off his eyebrows, hoping they would grow back bushier. He first contracted gonorrhea in 1847. He was once bitten on the face by a bear. He became a vegetarian in 1885. To make himself interesting, he occasionally bowed backward. (CL, p. 43)

Exceptional as these facts are, they can probably be found in any biography of Leo Tolstoy. There, however, they would be couched within a narrative of so many conventional items that their special nature might not be appreciated—surely not in the way that they strike the reader here, cut off as they are, in Beckettian fashion, from any consequential, didactic, or even conceptual order. It is as close as one might come to Burroughs's cut-up method without fully abandoning a sense of focus. And focus there surely is, as across the page the collagist's little Napoleon gazes up at that imposing face that in turn regards us so penetratingly as we skim these details from his life.

Barthelme's method, both with graphics and with words, has served to isolate these elements all the better for appreciating their new sense of compositional play. As other sentences and graphic "combines" take their place on subsequent pages, the reader is able to place Tolstoy in perspective (the story ends with a negative image of his face located at the point of infinity in an early draftsman's experiment with perspective). The final effect is conventional enough, that of sharing Tolstoy's art; and even though Barthelme's method has tempered that respect with humor, both in collages and in outright jokes (vast quantities of handkerchiefs for weeping, an architectural sense that the building is about to fall on you as an impression of Tolstoy's moral authority), the result is as full an appreciation as might be achieved in the most traditional stories, yet without relying on tradition for that effect.

"Brain Damage" is something else entirely. Using the same materials, it manipulates them toward a more abstract purpose, and on Barthelme's sliding critical scale would be closer to Burroughs's aggression than to Beckett's light-hearted play. Its initial sentence locates the narrator reading a book found in a garbage dump—in the first dump of several to be explored—and anticipating its rich life of promise. The experience that follows, however rich in accumulated sense of texture, does not cohere in any conventionally satisfactory way. Nature encountered here is alien and confused; for most of a page the narrator and his friends debate whether or not to plug in some beautiful flowers and fill them with electricity. Then come the collaged elements: a list in headline-size type of crowd reactions, a display of severed heads atop pedestals, another narrative paragraph (with its own collagelike descriptions of a waiter's funeral, the body cooked and garnished like a trout fillet), and then more headlines. The story proceeds with a steady rhythm of self-contained paragraphs, headlines, and collages, including a confession about the narrator's incompetent work as a newspaper reporter (misspelling names, garbling facts) and a Borgesian account of a strange people called the Wapituil whose world looks much like ours but only has one thing of each:

> We found that they lose interest very quickly. For instance they are fully industrialized, but they don't seem interested in taking advantage of it. After the steel mill produced the ingot, it was shut down. They

can conceptualize but they don't follow through. For instance, their week has seven days—Monday, Monday, Monday, Monday, Monday, Monday, and Monday. They have one disease, mononucleosis. The sex life of a Wapituil consists of a single experience, which he thinks about for a long time. (CL, p. 140)

While by itself this section is no different in kind from the passages in "Paraguay," its position as part of a collage story invites a special kind of reception by the reader. Though not causally related to the preceding paragraph on the narrator's checkered career in journalism, and in fact separated from it by a set of headlines and a full-page engraving of Prometheus bound, the juxtaposition might well prompt the reader to question the legitimacy of these reported details, strange as they are. Yet their internal sequence is self-generating, a kind of game the author can play in a manner that delights any reader able to discern the rules and anticipate what can happen next. What starts as apparent silliness ("They have a Museum of Modern Art and a telephone and a Martini, one of each") soon devolves upon its own system of order, and it is this order that yields the quite logical consequences of the paragraph, ending as it does with a rude but extremely effective joke.

Before it concludes, the story wanders across other junklike elements of our culture, including a university constructed entirely of three-mile-high sponges. Here one can see a progress under way suggestive of *The Dead Father*:

> "What is that very large body with hundreds and hundreds of legs moving across the horizon from left to right in a steady, carefully considered line?"
>
> "That is the tenured faculty crossing to the other shore on the plane of feasibility." (CL, p. 143)

When a headline asks "TO WHAT END?" (CL, p. 145), the narrator embraces his theme. "Oh there's brain damage in the east, and brain damage in the west, and upstairs there's brain damage, and downstairs there's brain damage, and in my lady's parlor—brain damage." Yet such damage may not be a liability, for the reluctance to connect the otherwise unconnectable has prevented narrator and reader from smoothing over the specific character of postmodern life with narcoticlike associations and other false transitions, just as the singular quality of life among the Wapituil allows the concentrated appreciation of each experience, even that of sex. As a result, Barthelme is able to take his reader "skiing along on the soft surface of brain damage, never to sink, because we don't understand the danger" (CL, p. 146); the real danger would be to sink into presumed meanings when the lack of logical connections prevents them.

The quest for new and exciting subjects that had proved so exhausting in *Unspeakable Practices, Unnatural Acts* is relieved in *City Life* by the author's more developed attitude toward such subjects, which for a time becomes one of irony. Because of this collection's prominence—the first of Barthelme's books to go into a third printing, be reviewed on the first page of the *New York Times Book Review*, and be selected by the Book of the Month Club—its tone became conclusive for critics who wished to recover this writer's work for the realistic tradition. Irony can be said to accept the premises of an object or a condition by critiquing it on its own terms, just as a subject being parodied is flattered by virtue of its selection. By this analysis, Barthelme would be little more than an up-to-date Perelman or even Benchley, using his position as a *New Yorker* regular to fashion bright and witty barbs directed at the foibles of a culture the writer actually lives in—and is nourished by—all too comfortably. Such a view ignores Barthelme's adversarial stance toward the basis of what his fiction ironizes. His earlier stories and even most of those collected in *City Life* direct their ironic comments not so much toward a subject as to the system that underlies it; like Roland Barthes', Donald Barthelme's argument is not with a specific practice but with the basic ignorance or disavowal of the systems that generate such practices. What certain persons in his culture believe is natural, Barthelme enjoys showing is artificial; what is presumed to be central is revealed as peripheral; and, most importantly, what is claimed to hold meaning is stripped bare to reveal its status as the product of purely systematic operations.

A thematic reference within "Kierkegaard Unfair to Schlegel" explains Barthelme's interest in irony. Within the story's interlocutary structure this exchange takes place:

Q: You are an ironist.
A: It's useful.
Q: How is it useful? (CL, p. 86)

The respondent then explains at great length, in a virtual essay on the subject, how making a joke about something functionally annihilates it (he finds a house stuffed to the rafters with play equipment, signaling that its inhabitants are bored; he quips that the remedy is worse than the disease, and by so doing cancels out the situation of boredom). From Kierkegaard's treatise he cites the nature of irony:

> Kierkegaard says that the outstanding feature of irony is that it confers upon the ironist a subjective freedom. The subject, the speaker, is negatively free. If what the ironist says is not his meaning, or is the opposite of his meaning, he is free both in relation to others and in relation to himself. He is not bound by what he has said. Irony is a means of depriving the object of its reality in order that the subject may feel free. (CL, pp. 87–88)

Reality is thus canceled when the ironist says something about the object that he doesn't mean: "Regarded in an ironical light, the object shivers, shatters, disappears" (CL, p. 88). Barthelme's use of irony emulates this approach and intends its effect; in it may be found the basic elements of deconstruction.

The use Barthelme devises for his irony and especially the direction in which he takes it become apparent in his next collection, Sadness, especially in its initial story, "Critique de la Vie Quotidienne." In this critique of the supposedly perfect life, the narrator manages to detail the realistic surfaces of middle class life and then systematically dismantle them, leaving nothing in their wake but a boozy void. Critics allied with the tradition will cite a long line of realists in The New Yorker's pages, from John O'Hara and John Cheever to Raymond Carver, whose stories do much the same thing. Their critiques of life, however, are based on manners—and not even manners as semiotic elements in a syntax of grammatical action, but as shorthand references to points of behavior the readers will recognize from their own lives, making for no structural difference between the fiction narrated and everyday gossip being exchanged. Barthelme, however, is interested only in the surfaces of this behavior, for that is where its signal value lies: as a dictionary of signs whose function as a language generates an infinite series of actions, the most interesting of which the author can arrange for us on the page.

What happens in "Critique de la Vie Quotidienne" is a demonstration of semiotic play at its best. The narrator begins by locating himself and (principally) his wife in relation to the magazines they read (all glossy surface) and the life styles they derive from them. She peruses *Elle* and fashions herself according to its suggestions for diet, decorating, and personal appearance. He loses himself in the *Journal of Sensory Deprivation* as he blots out the world with alcohol, his "nine drinks lined up there on the side of the table in soldierly array" (S, p. 4). All is measured out in a narrative as cautiously orderly as a Robbe-Grillet paragraph marks the progress of a sunlight ray across the floor. But unlike the nouveau romancier's story, Barthelme's tale is not reductive. There is no need to gird oneself against anthropomorphic projections, for his family's world is generated by flat, lifeless surfaces themselves, complete to that most typical of disruptions, their child's desire for a horse.

When the father's patient explanation (as patient as his systematic lining up of drinks) fails to satisfy, he ventures his own disruption, critiquing his wife for "visiting this outrageous child" on him (S, p. 6), and unleashes a torrent of disorder. Within one cascading sentence his wife has stormed from the room and dumped dinner (his other point of inquiry) on the kitchen floor, leaving him nothing but a few more iceless, above-his-limit drinks in which to find a truce with his circumstances. The joke has not been just on him, however, but on those circumstances that irony has systematically dismantled until, like the night's dinner, they no longer exist as such.

What opens the way toward a more extended form of narrative is not just the theme but the technical style such attention to deconstructive signification achieves. Following the flashy business with the grown-up's magazines, the child's cartoonlike desire for a horse, and the syntactic collision course followed by man and wife, Barthelme's narrator draws back to recount a thoroughly unexceptional episode from family life, unexceptional in everything but the carefully regulated way in which it is told. Like the work of Robbe-Grillet, it is strictly phenomenological, but even more so; its tightness with the facts themselves allows the readers to appraise for themselves the volcano of rage that lies beneath the surface, a volcano whose inevitable eruption is plot enough for the longest of stories:

> I remember once we were sleeping in a narrow bed, Wanda and I, in a hotel, on a holiday, and the child crept into bed with us.
>
> "If you insist on overburdening the bed," we said, "you must sleep at the bottom, with the feet." "But I don't want to sleep with the feet," the child said. "Sleep with the feet," we said, "they won't hurt you." "The feet kick," the child said, "in the middle of the night." "The feet or the floor," we said. "Take your choice." "Why can't I sleep with the heads," the child asked, "like everybody else?" "Because you are a child," we said, and the child subsided, whimpering, the final arguments in the case having been presented and the verdict in. But in truth the child was not without recourse; it urinated in the bed, in the vicinity of the feet. "God damn it," I said, inventing this formulation at the instant of need. "What the devil is happening, at the bottom of the bed?" "I couldn't help it," the child said. "It just came out." "I forgot to bring the plastic sheet," Wanda said. "Holy hell," I said, "Is there to be no end to this family life?" (S, p. 7)

Having set the terms for his narrative—that of semiotic factors at play within a strictly controlled system—Barthelme can turn back to the most mundane of circumstances and make it as novel, exciting, and amusing as any of his more bizarre constructions from earlier collections. Most of the passage consists of dialogue, a form more secure from the tamperings of personalist art, and even its positionings are limited to the same term, "said," to avoid any coloring not inherent to the material itself. What the characters discuss is strictly limited, and their dialogue sticks to the same incantatory phrases—the bed, the feet, and so forth. Throughout the passage rhythms establish themselves and are sustained; when a change occurs, such as the child quieting down, the narrator reflects it through a calming pace and subtle shift in diction (to a form of legalese). Words and rhythms are thus contained within the paragraph, its action being self-generated. When there is a disruption, all three parties at once reach for an internal justification, the father qualifying his expletive as a spontaneous invention, the child insisting its own problem "just came out," the wife closing in the circle by remembering she's neglected to supply any way out of it.

The potentials for an extended work such as *The Dead Father* are now evident, for Barthelme can suggest an interesting enough situation but also clear the way to expand it without the need for new marvels on every page, for the expansion will be generated by the same possibilities that have made the initial statement of situation. It is now just a case of finding the proper situation. For this, Barthelme was always exploring. Fragments of false starts appear here and there as stories in his collections: the Perpetua narratives, the Edward and Pia stories, still others with a pair named Henrietta and Alexandra, plus a *Comment* piece from *The New Yorker* of 13 June 1970, parts of which resurface in "A Film" and "The Flight of Pigeons from the Palace" in *Sadness* and in "Two Hours to Curtain" in *Guilty Pleasures*. Yet the greater thrust of the stories in these two collections is toward stating and investigating the issues that will make *The Dead Father* so necessary to the author's canon.

The shorter takes of *Sadness* and especially those gathered in *Guilty Pleasures* (shaped and presented as they are in parody and satire) give excellent indications of what has been on Donald Barthelme's mind as he approaches his second and most ambitious novel. Unlike the steady stream of advances in the first three collections, neither breaks vastly new technical ground. Rather, like the concluding story of *Unspeakable Practices, Unnatural Acts*, they entertain certain issues that are especially vexing to the author living and working within his culture. For those who would cast Barthelme primarily as a satirist, here lies the greatest field of topical material.

Yet consistent among those topics is the role of art within such social life, with the emphasis on the aesthetic end of such consideration. For every facet of daily existence that the author critiques, there is a writerly principle being analyzed; if this be Perelman or Benchley, it is a *New Yorker* hand at work in a private corner of the studio rather than on display at the Algonquin. And in nearly every case, the artistic business is more interesting than the social; without it, the commentary would be of another order entirely, along the lines collected a few years later in a small press edition, *Here in the Village*.

What can artistic imagination do for reordering the world's banalities into a more rewarding life? As in nearly all of his collections, Barthelme has at least one observation to make about the formally imaginative system that organized his own early years, that of Roman Catholicism. He appreciates its litanies and can even enjoy the self-absorption and eternal generation of its systematic terminology, but when figuring that a priest at confession hears no less than "forty-nine thousand one hundred and forty" adulteries confessed during his years of service, then "one wonders: Perhaps there should be a redefinition?" (S, p. 123). Psychology, one of the modern world's successors to organized religion, is similarly debated, particularly when an analyst does more harm than good in attempting to treat an artist, who needs no help at all in avoiding failure because "what an artist does, is fail. . . . The paradigmatic artistic experience is that of failure. The actualization fails to meet, equal, the intuition. There is something 'out there' which cannot be brought 'here' " (S, p. 93).

As alternatives to art need to be redefined, so do the uses of art themselves when faced with the current world. Thus Paul Klee can appreciate the beauty of camouflaged tarps hiding transported aircraft, forming seductive folds of hills and valleys, "the ropes the very essence of looseness, lapsing—it is irresistible" (S, p. 68). But when a plane he's guarding is lost or stolen, he uses another painterly talent—forgery, a form of graphic allusion—to change the manifest and make himself appear innocent. Other Barthelme characters risk their lives of art by constructing vehicles of complacency ("Subpoena") or letting themselves be swamped by the familiar, as in "The Temptation of St. Anthony" when the story identifies his greatest temptation as "ordinary life" (S, p. 154). "The Flight of Pigeons from the Palace," part of a fragmentary novel reworked in several different short stories, is a collage piece addressing the problem of artists forever struggling to entertain their audiences with new aesthetic wonders, and includes a comment any skeptical critic could have addressed to Barthelme's own regular progress through a decade's volume of *The New Yorker*:

It is difficult to keep the public interested.
The public demands new wonders piled on new wonders.

Often we don't know where our next marvel is coming from.

The supply of strange ideas is not endless.

The development of new wonders is not like the production of canned goods. Some things appear to be wonders in the beginning, but when you become familiar with them, are not wonderful at all. Sometimes a seventy-five-foot highly paid cacodemon will raise only the tiniest frisson. Some of us have even thought of folding the show— closing it down. That thought has been gliding through the hallways and rehearsal rooms of the show. (S, p. 139)

Yet this penultimate paragraph only sets up the promise of the story's concluding sentence, "The new volcano we have just placed under contract seems very promising . . ." (S, p. 139). Carrying on is the least one can do, if daily life stands any chance of being transformed into the ideal. "The self cannot be escaped," the story titled "Daumier" concludes, "but it can be, with ingenuity and hard work, distracted. There are always openings, if you can find them, there is always something to do" (S, p. 183). Significantly it is the volume's single previously unpublished piece, "Träumerei," that makes the most extensive test of existing artworks against the quotidian progress of this life.

The most impressive result of such ingenuity and hard work is The Dead Father, published three years after "Daumier." But as a short fictionist Barthelme could still show that his culture abounded with strange ideas and marvels subject only to a talented writer's ability to display them. Such demonstrations are more often deft little object exercises, more like the brief essays of Roland Barthes' Mythologies than the extended investigations of his Système de la Mode; perhaps to distinguish how his own short stories do more than just illustrate such effects, Barthelme collects eleven years' of these writings into a separate volume, Guilty Pleasures, and adds a preface distinguishing them as parodies, satires, and—most generally—as "simple expressions of stunned wonder at the fullness and mysteriousness" of our public life, a characterization worthy of Roland Barthes' writing as well (GP, p. [vii]). As with Barthes, Barthelme's introduction to a broadly popular audience came from such work—his first appearance in The New Yorker is with a piece collected here, "L'Lapse," and through the middle 1960s his nonfictive commentaries on such topics as foreign films, advertising, and other magazines' styles continued to appear in this journal almost as frequently as his more systematically collected short stories.

The organization of *Guilty Pleasures* is itself a critical act, and justifies Barthelme's decision to hold these pieces back from his earlier collections until they could be massed and structured for effect. The two dozen contributions are grouped in sections, unlabeled except for numbers but conforming to three distinct and artistically progressive practices: stylistic analysis, imitation, and transcription. The first identifies a practice; the second adopts it; and the third, closest to Barthelme's fully developed fiction, creates a narrative by transcribing the style itself as an event (no small achievement in a world whose attention moves almost at once to the objects style represents). Traditional parody thus recedes, surviving long enough for the peculiar feature of language usage to be identified but keeping the way clear for the author to construct his own short story from its materials.

In the first section, Barthelme draws his reader's attention to the stylistic idiosyncracies of several magazines—*Consumer Reports, Cosmopolitan, Time,* and *Newsweek*—and of an odd triumvirate of writers: the nineteenth-century novelist Honoré de Balzac, the filmmaker Michelangelo Antonioni, and the pop anthropologist Carlos Castaneda. What draws them together is not just their popularity as purveyors of texts, but the identifiable popularity of their style. In a few cases, Barthelme's own contribution is minimal. "Snap Snap" begins with a page and a half of epigraphs, every one of them using the word "snapped" to identify a news figure's quote; the four-page story that follows begins as the complaint of a colorless writer who despairs of such snappy style, but which trails off after two pages into another list of quotes being "cried" and then "warned." As a literary technique, Barthelme's achievement is little more than the standard *New Yorker* column filler, reprinting and making fun of some other journal's silliness with words. "That Cosmopolitan Girl" takes off from one of that magazine's advertisements and concocts a four-page narrative punctuated by (and almost completely consisting of) the exclamation marks, rhetorical questions, and incessant underscorings that make rapt emphasis its own subject.

But with the other stories from this initial grouping Barthelme rises from the parodist's satisfied amusement and draws forth a true narrative from these quirks. In "Down the Line with the Annual" he presents a narrator whose life has been stunted and blocked by a text he has encountered—not a dream about his own evil nature or a devilish scene stumbled upon in the night, but the month-by-month product evaluations in *Consumer Reports*. Taken up with its own function and existing as it does within its own language of destructive testing, this style nevertheless offers a picture that, as a world view, is devastating:

> The world is sagging, snagging, scaling, spalling, pilling, pinging, pitting, warping, checking, fading, chipping, cracking, yellowing, leaking, staling, shrinking, and in dynamic unbalance, and there is mildew to think about, and ruptures and fractures of internal organs from lap belts, and substandard brake fluids, and plastic pipes alluring to rats, and transistor radios whose estimated battery life, like the life of man, is a feeble, flickering thing. (GP, p. 6)

Much more than just parodying his subject, Barthelme takes its words—words which might never occur in a context other than product evaluation—and runs them together in a litany of consumer evils. Individually, they are the nuisances and vexations of a householder; together, they are a nightmare vision, sweeping over the reader in waves of sonority and accumulative ruin. As the terms pass by, one catches fleeting glimpses of paint, siding, appliances, and automobiles gone to ruin. And because so much of contemporary life is lived within their bounds, that too becomes a devastating prospect whose conclusively expanding rhythm takes in the full meaning of life—which, in the story's original appearance (*New Yorker*, 21 March 1964: 34–35), is characterized in the words of Thomas Hobbes as "nasty, brutish, and short." From this linguistic environment Barthelme builds not just an inventory of effects but a convincing narrative in which the narrator's own life falls apart as systematically as any gadget being tested at the magazine, reminding readers that the culture we have made is what we now are.

In similar fashion "L'Lapse" outlines a film scenario in the new-wave gestures that create an entire (if decidedly posed and off-center) universe, just as the awkwardly mannered situations typical of Balzac can themselves form a comically fragmented narrative in "Eugénie Grandet" (another reminder of the author's affinity for Roland Barthes' use of lexemes as units of narrative meaning). The funniest of these stylistic parodies is "The Teachings of Don B.: A Yankee Way of Knowledge," which right from its deft transposition of Carlos Castaneda's title, *The Teachings of Don Juan: A Yaqui Way of Knowledge*, proves capable of substituting the most personally mundane details of Don Barthelme in his Greenwich Village habitat for the exotic doings of the sorcerer Don Juan in northern Mexico. For all of Castaneda's business with magic and wonders, the true substance of his books and their readerly effectiveness can be found in the tone of awe in which otherwise unexceptional events are recounted; by shifting person and place to the most familiar elements available—Barthelme's own *vie quotidienne* detailed in the initial story of *Sadness*—the critique becomes thoroughly convincing.

In the volume's second section Barthelme, always envious of painters, uses a contemporary movement's fondness for pastiche and gesture to "do" versions of certain classics, such as *Washington Crossing the Delaware* (already "done" once in a reprise by painter Larry Rivers) and the witticisms of Ogden Nash. As with Rivers's style of painting, such "doing" fills a canvas with one's own techniques even as the subject matter takes care of itself, thanks to its existence not as something out there in the real world but as a reference within the reader's knowledge of art. At the time, critics ventured that the subject of art might well become art history, and in these pieces Barthelme takes fiction down that same path. But only to a certain point, for when the presentation of language becomes interesting enough as its own subject, then the author can take those twists of words and phrases as existing elements (just like the image of Washington in the boat's prow, making his way across the wintry river toward his place in destiny) and use them to generate something not familiar or boring at all: a new story.

Such innovation is based on a practice that gives this collection its title, drawn from Barthelme's confession in the book's preface that some of these pieces "are pretexts for the pleasure of cutting up and pasting together pictures, a secret vice gone public. Guilty pleasures are the best"

(*GP*, p. [vii]). Only three stories use actual pictures, and in one case simply for an initial illustration (ancient stoneware described as NASA's first photo of the human soul), in another ("The Expedition") primarily for caption material, with just a few reordered for collage. Full-fledged cutting and pasting is restricted to "A Nation of Wheels," Barthelme's wittiest use of such materials, in which the title's dead metaphor is brought back to life by selecting a broad range of engravings from the nineteenth century and inserting gigantic automobile tires clipped from today's advertisements, implying that these wheels dominate everything.

The most effective cutting and pasting among the third set of stories involves language, especially those situations which seem defined by a peculiar grammar and syntax. The rigamarole of duties and conduct for Playboy bunnies is an obvious target, as is the catalog of an open university; both subjects not only concern themselves with interests and problems not even existing in the outside world, but have their own overdeveloped systems of meanings bred within the hermetic confines of a system absolutely self-contained. A Playboy club and a hippie-dippy university extension program are removed from the day-to-day world, and so Barthelme's readers can enjoy the superiority of looking into them from above and being amused by the idiosyncracies of their operation. But something like the Ed Sullivan Show, one of the most popular television programs of all time, is more familiar, for years part of a majority of American households' Sunday nights, and therefore when the author can display the hermetic workings of its own syntax the effect can be disarming.

"And Now Let's Hear It for the Ed Sullivan Show!" the title announces, emulating the show's ambience and tenor. Describing it is a task suitable for Barthelme's tight-lipped phenomenological style that had worked so well with the quotidian scenes in *Sadness*, here isolating the syntactic oddness that would otherwise sweep past the viewer in a wash of familiarity:

> The Ed Sullivan Show. Sunday night. Church of the unchurched. Ed stands there. He looks great. Not unlike an older, heavier Paul Newman. Sways a little from side to side. Gary Lewis and the Playboys have just got off. Very strong act. Ed clasps hands together. He's introducing somebody in the audience. Who is it? Ed points with his left arm. "Broken every house record at the Copa," Ed says of the man he's

introducing. Who is it? It's . . . Don Rickles! Rickles stands up. Eyes glint. Applause. "I'm gonna make a big man outta you!" Ed says. Rickles hunches a shoulder combatively. Eyes glint. Applause. Jerry Vale introduced. Wives introduced. Applause. "When Mrs. Sullivan and I were in Monte Carlo (pause, neatly suppressed belch), "we saw them" (pause, he's talking about the next act), "for the first time and signed them instantly! The Kuban Cossacks! Named after the River Kuban!" (GP, pp. 101–2)

Hung out to dry on Barthelme's bare-bones structure, the doings of the Ed Sullivan Show are exposed for what they are: awkwardly segued parcels of an entertainment staggering from one overhyped wonder to another, no statement capable of standing without an exclamation point and all of it held together by little more than the host's self-centered posturings. That the program's nature is as choppily cut and pasted as Barthelme's own technique is a happy reinforcement. The major effect, however, is that of transcribing Sullivan's doings to show how idiosyncratic they are, and how these idiosyncracies have come together to form a grammar and syntax that can generate such shows, Sunday after Sunday, ad infinitum. A Jetstar typewriter commercial, a musical number by Mary Hopkin, then cut to Perle Mesta in the audience—the Sullivan show exaggerates the cut-and-paste nature of TV technology, and so Barthelme's further step of narrating by transcription, making no excuses for Ed's ludicrous lack of transitions, is appropriately an extension in kind.

City Life, Sadness, and Guilty Pleasures collect stories that address Barthelme's culture on its own terms. Not quite junk sculpture, these efforts are more in line with Robert Rauschenberg's combines, three-dimensional assemblages of bits and pieces from the current world that not only make a topical reference but are put together in a way that emulates that world's peculiar way of functioning in producing a new work of art. The method is not just one of parody or satire; those practices are helpful in finding a subject, but even to get the art process under way the author must look further to identify and understand the situation's generative grammar, and then use that grammar to produce something that both comments on the original situation and yields a work beyond it.

By the end of 1974, with well over one hundred stories published and what he considered the best of them collected in six volumes, Donald Barthelme continued to feel challenged by the prospect of longer narrative. His *New Yorker* writing had established him as one of the era's leading innovators in short fiction, but his first novel, *Snow White*, had been praised only on those same terms: a brilliance of specific effect and a dazzling ability to entertain with a quick succession of fragments. Could there be a subject appropriate to the full length of a novel yet amenable to such handling as his fiction in shorter forms had perfected? Could the same aesthetic issues as debated and transformed in the collections from *Come Back, Dr. Caligari* to *Guilty Pleasures* survive treatment in a work lasting two hundred pages rather than ten? Around him, artists were making such moves, Andy Warhol investigating the nature of paintings in series and Robert Rauschenberg proceeding from singular combines to more narrative treatments in silkscreened canvases. With *The Dead Father* Barthelme takes a similar step, realizing that the test would be not just how much longer a distance he could travel but how much of his first decade of literary innovation he could take along for the ride.

Chapter Four

The Novels

_____

With his canon complete, Barthelme's relation to the novel can be understood as clearly as his position on the aesthetic issues that prompted his reinvention of short story technique in the earliest phase of his career. Even though he turned to a quite different form, the historical/allegorical romance, just before his death, the three novels he did publish make an analytical statement thanks to their even distribution throughout his three decades of work—*Sadness* coming near the start, *The Dead Father* almost precisely at the center, and *Paradise* near the end.

The books themselves are studied best in sequence, for they tell as much about the author's development as a novelist as the progress of his first several collections make evident about his work with the short story. Those stories, to be sure, forged new ground, reinventing the rules and changing the goals for a genre that had been quite stable through at least three generations of success, beginning with the masterpieces of F. Scott Fitzgerald and continuing, in the same *New Yorker* pages Barthelme was to inherit, with the socially mannered work of John O'Hara, John Cheever, and John Updike. Here was a field ripe for disruption. But in terms of larger critical and especially theoretical effect, the story form itself was not the heart of the issue. No one in the late 1950s and early 1960s was talking about "the death of the short story," but the death of the novel was so popular and vehemently debated an issue that Ronald Sukenick could, just a few years later, make a statement by using the term to title his novella and first collection, *The Death of the Novel and Other Stories* (1969).

The radical nature of Barthelme's success with shorter forms actually made his task with the novel harder, for in handling certain aesthetic issues—replacing the imitation of an action with a writerly action in itself, making his narrative be an object rather than be about one, disrupting the preconceived readings that use fictive elements as shorthand cues to imagined consequences, defamiliarizing such readings by humor and surprise, reviving attention on almost every page with some new technical marvel—he was fragmenting the more expansive properties of his work. Nearly every technique developed in his first six collections serves to concentrate and even purify the reader's view, making associations more of a hopscotch affair than an orderly progress along a developing sequence. An average passage from these early works is like a collage: instead of prompting the reader to turn the page, the author provides more than enough internal action, of parts relating to parts and the overall plan reflecting back upon itself, so that the interplay of subject and syntax retains its own identity. There is a great deal of action, but almost always in one place; and even moving from page to page in a single short story is like skipping from object to object in an Ernst collage or Cornell box, where the component elements retain their own identity even as they contribute to an overall effect.

Snow White, published in 1967 as the author's second book, follows right in line with Barthelme's development as a short story writer, for it uses most of the techniques introduced in *Come Back, Dr. Caligari* and anticipates their propoundings as themes in *Unspeakable Practices, Unnatural Acts*; plus there are pages of headline type in ranks that will appear a bit later in the title story of *City Life*. Though no chapters are numbered, the novel's 181 pages are broken up into over 100 chapterlike segments, set off by space and starting fresh at the page top with the initial word capitalized. Each segment has its center: a character, a locale, or a specific action. There is a progress among them, but one that moves in jumps and jerks, like blackouts in a comedy review as different members of the cast take center stage and spotlight for their individual bit or turn. Within these passages the narrative is presented in Barthelme's clipped, understated manner that isolates each element of semiotic syntax all the more, as in this passage where one of the dwarfs, returning from work, thinks about his date with Snow White that night:

> Henry walked home with his suit in a plastic bag. He had been washing the buildings. But something was stirring in him, a wrinkle in the

groin. He was carrying his bucket, too, and his ropes. But the wrinkle in his groin was monstrous. "Now is necessary to court her, and win her, and put on this clean suit, and cut my various nails, and drink something that will kill the millions of germs in my mouth, and say something flattering, and be witty and bonny, and hale and kinky, and pay her a thousand dollars, all just to ease this wrinkle in the groin. It seems a high price." Henry let his mind stray to the groin. Then he let his mind stray to her groin. Do girls have groins? The wrinkle was still there. "The remedy of Origen. That is still open to one. That door, at least, has not been shut." (*SW*, pp. 64–65)

Such narration moves with the deliberate pace of phenomenology but remains interesting for the way its telling deadpans it through such twists and turns of thought. It is a style Barthelme finds effective for underscoring his theme, of how men (the dwarfs) are fascinated by but lost within the mysteries of woman (Snow White) and how woman's sense of disruption, not even fully understood by herself, becomes such a perplexing object that its very absence is nonetheless something that can be sensed as a rupture of syntax:

Perhaps we should not be sitting here and tending the vats and washing the buildings and carrying the money to the vault once a week, like everybody else. Perhaps we should be doing something else entirely, with our lives. God knows what. We do what we do without thinking. . . . It was worse before. That is something that can safely be said. It was worse before we found Snow White wandering in the forest. Before we found Snow White wandering in the forest we lived lives stuffed with equanimity. There was equanimity for all. We washed the buildings, tended the vats, wended our way to the county cathouse once a week (heigh-ho). Like everybody else. We were simple bourgeois. We knew what to do. When we found Snow White wandering in the forest, hungry and distraught, we said: "Would you like something to eat?" Now we do not know what to do. Snow White has added a dimension of confusion and misery to our lives. Whereas once we were simple bourgeois who knew what to do, now we are complex bourgeois who are at a loss. We do not like this complexity. We circle it wearily, prodding it with a shopkeeper's forefinger: What is it? Is it, perhaps, *bad for business*? Equanimity has leaked away. There was a moment, however, when equanimity was not the chief consideration. That moment in which we looked at Snow White and understood for the first time that we were fond of her. That was a moment. (*SW*, pp. 87–88)

The passage is effective because of its self-contained and internally re-generative nature. The speaker's careful pace makes the words graspable like concrete objects and repeatable as physical forces within the sentence—note how *bourgeois* is almost literally handed about and reshaped as a notion, how *bad for business* takes on materiality as something quite real in such worlds, and how *equanimity*, otherwise an abstract concept, becomes so palpable. The dwarfs' encounter with Snow White, recalled from the past, becomes a solid reality thanks to its rote repetition (which draws attention to itself as a phrase physically present in the paragraph's language). Mentioned just once, these subjects would make a very short passage indeed; but because they exist in a loop, a page-long paragraph is generated that gives fair approximation of the dwarfs' emotional state.

How Barthelme's interest in these materials runs to novel length is a consequence of the form itself: postmodernizing the most traditional of fairy tales. Although the Grimms' version is printable as a short story, its effect is that of an oral tale, and as such boasts the bedtime capability of seemingly endless extension at the same time its careful structure of rise, fall, and redemption rewards listeners for their attention throughout so many digressions and delays. Then there is the Disney version—another special variety of extension, for while its nature is short (the cartoon) its treatment is feature length. When in 1967 Donald Barthelme offers his rendition, it is received in several contexts, including not just the Grimms' and Disney's tellings but in a smart, sassy, and disruptive world which has discarded both the classic fairy tale and the Disney film as respected forms.

The narrative of a postmodern Snow White, then, calls for more time and space than a 4,000-word short story. But the way Barthelme retells his tale also demands greater length. The contrast between his work and those of his predecessors is made by more than just context, for Snow White and her seven admirers are not only dropped into a wild sixtiesish Greenwich Village scene but have their manners of behavior changed as well, all of which takes time to be established. Other updatings of the story are even further reaching, and include the narrative's language and poses. There is a discernible style to the words and situations of a Grimm Brothers tale—recognizing them is an important part of their effect, and few children will accept such bedtime stories that do not soothe them into sleep with a certain regularity of measure and familiarity of shape. What Walt Disney did to storytelling is even more apparent, and controversial enough to inspire Richard Schickel's impassioned critique, *The Disney Version* (New York: Simon and Schuster, 1968), which charges that the filmmaker denied the mystery of nature by anthropomorphizing it and ignored the even greater possibilities of humankind by trivializing it into clichés and copying outdated imitations of life. Barthelme's *Snow White*, of course, exists within the presence of these two earlier tellings, and there is no way the author could make even the simplest narrative statement without having it rebound among such readerly influences and perhaps—if we are to believe Schickel—against Disney-inspired blocks within Barthelme's consciousness as well. But because the 1967 novel emulates the style not just of the Grimms and Walt Disney but of the author of *Come Back, Dr. Caligari* as well, a broader canvas becomes an absolute necessity.

It is the book's clever use of language and poses that marks it so clearly as Barthelme's work, and also lets it comment on the limitations of the Grimms and Disney even as it steps beyond them. The language is such as never spoken in a fairy tale or feature length cartoon: that of contemporary philosophy, vaguely European in cast, which like the existential ponderings of "Me and Miss Mandible" both makes fun of the form and draws some thematic impact. It is no small joke to see the dwarfs, who are colorless, task-oriented functionaries in the Grimms' version and cuddlesomely cute, harmless figures of low comedy for Walt Disney, speak like Maurice Merleau-Ponty convening with the philosophy department at the Collège de France. Even funnier is how that language is then undercut by the poses from which it is delivered: that of hilarious ineptitude, in which the painfully cautious conjugations of European thought are splayed across the page in broad Americanese. Consider a dwarf's instruction to his colleagues on how to deal with the fetching but ungraspable beauty of the woman they love:

> Now, what do we apprehend when we apprehend Snow White? We apprehend, first, two three-quarter-scale breasts floating toward us wrapped, typically, in a red towel. Or, if we are apprehending her from the other direction, we apprehend a beautiful snow-white arse floating away from us wrapped in a red towel. Now I ask you: What, in these two quite distinct apprehensions, is the constant? The factor that remains the same? Why, quite simply, the red towel. I submit that, rightly understood, the problem of Snow White has to do at its center with nothing else but *red towels*. Seen in this way, it immediately becomes a non-problem. We can easily dispense with the slippery and untrustworthy and expensive effluvia that is Snow White, and cleave instead to the towel. That is my idea, gentlemen. And I have here in this brown bag . . . I have taken the liberty of purchasing . . . here, Edward, here is your towel . . . Kevin . . . Clem . . ." Chang watched sourly. That was the trouble with being a Chinese. Too much detachment. "I don't want a ratty old red towel. *I want the beautiful snow-white arse itself!*" (*SW*, pp. 100–101)

The language is comic because of who is saying it and how it is said, with the same repetitions and loopings Barthelme has used so well elsewhere in this novel and in his short stories. But as a thematic pose, it becomes doubly effective, for the whole philosophic notion of relying on the carefully measured use of language to reason out a problem is completely exploded by Chang's deconstructive complaint. The patiently restated theorems sound as if the speaker is walking on thin ice—this the reader senses quite easily, and like the proverbial child at bedtime can anticipate the inevitable cracking up of this over-fine system and the speaker's plunge into the chilly waters of the abyss below.

Much of the novel's action takes place within this linguistic framework. The dwarfs spend most of their passages contemplating such things as "withdrawal" and "retraction" (*SW*, pp. 4, 13), while Snow White herself confesses dismay in her first line: "Oh I wish there were some words in the world that were not the words I always hear!" (*SW*, p. 6). Those words do seem to be empty forms, her choice of breakfast cereals being from among the brightly colored boxes of Chix, Rats, and Fear, while the only way to counter her feeling of incompleteness, as she waits for her prince to come, is to survey the alternatives of Prince Philip, Prince Albert, Prince Valiant, and Prince Matchabelli. Bored with being "just" a housewife (or "*horsewife*," as the story puts it for emphasis), she at times blames the world for not being able to supply her a prince, but also realizes that the paltriness of such princes available, constructed as they are by the news and advertising media, is due to her own culture's inability to imagine something finer. That is why she remains with the dwarfs: because she cannot think of anything better to do.

This imaginative depletion extends to politics and society at large. The time is clearly the mid-1960s, with a counterculture divorced from its leadership but unable to create a new order on its own. The president of this land incarnates the linguistic habits of Lyndon Johnson, conducting the President's War on Poetry and speaking in rhythms redolent of LBJ's White House years ("I am concerned. . . . Because I am the President. Finally. The President of the whole fucking country. And they are Americans. My Americans" [*SW*, p. 81]). Even more indictably, his subjects adopt his own linguistic strategies, most notably the government jargon for conducting the war in Vietnam, as when the heroine's try at another style of fairy tale resolution, that of Rapunzel, fails, and is subjected to the analysis that "no one responded to Snow White's hair initiative" (*SW*, p. 141). The deeper reason is that, in this novel's view, Americans do not see themselves as princely. Yet even beyond this lies a question: is it the fault of people not to act princely, or of the world that expects them to? The latter consideration fits with Barthelme's larger critique of an outdated modernism confusing the issues in an otherwise postmodern world. In terms of the author's thematic progress, the dead father is not buried yet.

As Barthelme will demonstrate in *The Dead Father*, there is room for a great deal of valid cultural expression even as the father, still kicking, is dragged to his grave—just as that dragging takes up the length and breadth of the novel. For *Snow White*, that expression takes a more studied form, appropriate to the writer's first effort in the genre. If modern journalism, advertising, and politics have destroyed language, then the page is clear for the creation of new forms; and if linguistic forms create our sense of reality, then the way is open for a new world. Much of this first novel dramatizes such understanding, from the characters' sensitivity to metaphor, reacting to the sexual terminology for simple mechanics, to their appreciation of how the word is often more powerful than the idea. Language has the power to obfuscate; one remembers the realtime online computer-controlled wish evaporation from the story "Report." But in *Snow White* Barthelme prefers to play with its creative potential, such as proposing an electronic wastebasket that instead of sonic waves uses the sound of complex words, namely "an intimidation followed by a demoralization eventuating in a disintegration, one assumes" (*SW*, p. 129). Colorful language has its own action, and can take on its own life, such as when a dwarf admits that "I wanted to make a far-reaching evaluation. I had in mind launching a three-pronged assault, but the prongs wandered off seduced by fires and clowns" (*SW*, p. 53). Deadened terms can be brought back to life by little twists of defamiliarization, such as substituting "horsewife" for "housewife" and conducting passionate debates on the wisdom of "batting the baby" (allowing such gems as "Spare the bat and the child rots" [*SW*, p. 116] in which the rhythm alone carries authority).

What such clever use of language does is reawaken readers' attention, pointing out not just how much linguistic wool has been pulled over one's eyes but what a colorful world can be woven from a language reempowered by an alert imagination. In *Snow White*, this attention and re-creation is achieved at the expense of the characters and their narrative fortunes. They themselves are prisoners of *dreck*, that world of language where the "blanketing effect" (*SW*, p. 96) of meaningless patter becomes their full existence, appropriate enough in a society where the production of garbage is increasing at a ratio soon to be 100 percent. They even have a program and a name for it to accommodate such a state, placing them "on the leading edge of this trash phenomenon" (*SW*, p. 97). Still, there is an aesthetic advantage, for when the books they read have "a lot of *dreck* in them" they are forced not to look between the lines ("for there is nothing there, in those white spaces") but to read the lines themselves with the knowledge that they are devoid of referential content (*SW*, p. 106). Here is one way of making the work of fiction not be about something but be that something itself. True, for the dwarfs this new style of reading is accomplished at the cost of a rewarding existence, but theirs is not the life of the book. That life of fiction is being engendered by the experience of reading *Snow White*, and even as the subject of the book is a story of failure (the rescuing hero turns out to be "pure frog" and misses his cue by drinking the poison himself) the act of reading it is an artistic success.

Within Donald Barthelme's development as a novelist, *Snow White* stands as a statement of what he considers to be the problems, both formal and thematic—problems with both the novel and his culture. If this first work suggests what needs to be done, *The Dead Father* (1975) actually does it—clearing the way, eventually, for the unrestricted practice of novelistic expression in the aptly titled *Paradise* published as his third and conclusive effort in 1986, and allowing uncontested space for the delights of an allegorical romance before death closes the canon forever. Even at this second stage the going is much smoother, for the jerky fragmentation of the postmodern fairy tale with its hundred-plus segments relaxes a bit into twenty-three chapters (one of which frames a self-contained insert) spread out among about the same number of pages. The random diversity of Snow White's life among the seven dwarfs, her prince, and the evil witch is replaced by the centrality of the Dead Father and the struggle of his son and the two young women to haul him to his grave. The hauling itself is a much clearer line of development than the narrative distraction of *Snow White*, and there is much less need for passages discussing aesthetic principles behind the work; what commentary there is bears directly on the notion of fatherhood being laid to rest. Most apparent, and eventually most important, is the difference in style. Whereas *Snow White* demanded the playing out of deconstructive passages at length, such as the dwarfs' painstaking analyses of their condition in the manner of "Critique de la Vie Quotidienne," *The Dead Father* manages to be itself without elaborate demonstrations of how this can be possible. In a pleasantly simple way, the narrative just happens, the result of Barthelme's confidence gained from writing not just over one hundred stories but from completing an accomplished, full-length work, *Snow White*.

"Eleven o'clock in the morning. The sun doing its work in the sky" (DF, p. 6). These sentences that get the action under way do so without the need of an active verb. The words themselves are simply laid on the page as a material surface inert for the reader's examination. They are neither acting nor acted upon by anything within the narrative; all such action comes from the reading, which is allowed to appreciate the object Barthelme has offered to view.

The reading itself begins easily, almost elementally, as the narrative's line of progress stretches across the novel's plane. Beginning, middle, and end are clear from the start, as the task of hauling the Dead Father to his grave has only one possible destination, as inevitable as the progress of life itself. The cast of characters is similarly well defined and unified by that task. A group of men do the hauling, and only one of them is named, principally as a figure of comic relief (Edmund, with his drinking problem and generally proletarian airs). In charge is the son, Thomas, whose quietly adversarial relation to the Dead Father is enhanced by the more vocal complaints of the two young women, Julie and Emma. The most flamboyant figure by far is that of the Dead Father, who is not only the center of attention but the source of extreme behavior, colorful language, and complicating actions. What in *Snow White* was fragmented among the universe of topics spun off from the characters' already complex relations is here focused on a clear and simple action concerning a central character so dominant that his very presence is a signal of what needs to be done. As a tale, *The Dead Father* is virtually prototypical in form.

Part of this tale's appeal is the elemental nature of such a format, much like the minimalism of classic drama where a character's speech holds action enough to keep the larger narrative moving. In the Dead Father's case, this potency is an attribute of character—certainly as he views his own character, because to him speaking is the same as making something happen. He prides himself on ideas and imagination, expressed as a "certain artistry . . . in my ukases" (DF, p. 7). *Ukase* is the historic term for a czar's pronouncement, a statement that by its simple utterance becomes law and therefore a reality. The word is not only authoritarian but archaic, and also reflects upon itself by being a word whose voicing creates its existence not just as a sound but as a physical state of affairs. It is also a style of behavior compatible with the more domestic nature of fatherhood as Barthelme wishes to capture it in this novel, where the father's tyranny begins with the power he puts behind his statements, which often have no more sense to them than those of a monarchy in decay. The value to narrative clarity is considerable, because the Dead Father only needs to announce himself in order to provide a problem for the others (his dominance) and imply a solution (his silencing). The fact that he is already "dead" is no resolution, and indeed is the immediate cause of the problem, for—like the lingering presence of an aesthetically outdated modernism that bedevils so many of the characters in Barthelme's early stories and prompts the writerly disruption and invention of new forms—the old man clings to influence by virtue of his voice, an anxiety of influence the subsequent generation is only now trying to overcome. Quieting him down is a nuisance these younger folk have to deal with from page to page as they undertake to bury him, the only effective way of finding silence. Though physically dead, his presence lingers as a carcass not yet successfully interred, and the struggle with this presence is as much of a story as the physical hauling to the grave. But that actual hauling remains as the novel's clear linear structure, making the more philosophic theme all the more direct.

Snow White had divided up such philosophizing among the broodings, confessions, and pseudological demonstrations of the heroine herself and several of the dwarfs; these musings carried nearly all of Barthelme's themes, but were peripheral to the narrative's more basic action, that of Snow White being rescued (or, in this case, not rescued) by her prince. As statements, they were reactive rather than causal, and while giving readers explanations of why the characters were in such sorry predicaments did not emerge from the action itself—unless one were to accept Snow White as an intellectualized café novel where characters' reflective talk constitutes the story, which is certainly not the style of book Barthelme would have wished to write (if anything, his characters' behavior ridicules such forms). Now in The Dead Father the central figure's speech is a functional reality: it is because he speaks that there is a problem, it is the nature of his speech that makes it significant, and it is an archetypically narrative task to shut him up, involving as it does the protracted dragging of his body across the landscape to his grave, with the old man kicking and screaming (generating typical fatherly problems) all the way.

What are those problems? The major one is a resistance to giving up the stage. If Dead Fathers, like outmoded ideas, passed gently from the scene, there would be no need for such a long narrative to dispose of them. More immediately, there is the fatherly style of self-definition, which involves establishing his own stature by diminishing that of others (particularly of sons) and aggrandizing himself by outrageous actions (often involving killing and, by virtue of a randy interest in sex, *creating*—the terms the Dead Father uses are "slaying" and "fathering"). In characterizing these actions Barthelme displays his appealing talents for freshness and whimsy, taking the most apparently outrageous circumstance and showing how apt an expression of affairs it is. The Dead Father forces his son to dress in an orange cap tipped with silver bells and remain so costumed from age sixteen to sixty-five. It makes for quite an image, which Julie takes time to appreciate: "Brown-and-beige, maroon-and-gray, red-and-green," she observes of his idiotic cloak, "all bells chilattering. What a picture. I thought, What perfect fools" (*DF*, p. 7). Much later, Barthelme will concoct a similar preposterous circumstance, that of primates attending a sophisticated party, just so Thomas can accost Julie for her behavior: "I saw you dancing with that ape" (*DF*, p. 102), all as a way of reinvesting otherwise dead language with a new reality (and by doing so reminding readers what these words really mean).

Complementing such revivified language are the philosophical discussions of fatherhood. Unlike the detached ponderings of *Snow White*, these passages in *The Dead Father* are direct consequences of the narrative's action: after a particularly vexing instance of fatherly behavior, Thomas will question or complain, only to be put in his pseudological place by old dad. No matter what the subject, the Dead Father informs Thomas, he can never know—"Because you are not a father." When Thomas names a child he has indeed fathered, the old man quickly counters, "Doesn't count." Why not? Because "A son can never, in the fullest sense, become a father. Some amount of amateur effort is possible. A son may after honest endeavor produce what some people might call, technically, children. But he remains a son. In the fullest sense" (*DF*, p. 33). The Dead Father's transrationality describes quite well an emotional state, and the volatility of that state is what fuels the narrative action—which will, in turn, spark more comments on the nature of fatherhood.

Climaxing these discussions of fatherhood is the section "A Manual for Sons," set typographically within chapter 17. Like the novel itself, the manual has twenty-three sections, the effect of which is to concretize, in a helpfully instructional form, the issues that have propelled the narrative thus far and dictate the form of its conclusion. It begins with description—how fathers behave, how they can be controlled—but moves on to the emotional considerations the narrative had been able to dramatize but not explain. Now, through the voice of an anonymous social analyst, Barthelme is able to consider why the Dead Father remains so dominant and Thomas so ambivalent even as he hauls the old man to his grave. "The death of fathers: When a father dies, his fatherhood is returned to the All-Father, who is the sum of all dead fathers taken together," the manual explains. Thus fatherhood is denied the son, while he is left with "an inner voice commanding, haranguing, yes-ing and no-ing—a binary code, yes no yes no yes no yes no, governing your every, your slightest movement, mental or physical. At what point do you become yourself? Never, wholly, you are always part of him" (DF, p. 144). On the other hand, under the subject of patricide, we are advised that "patricide is a bad idea," both because it is illegal and because it proves the father's deepest accusations have been true. But most of all, "it is not necessary to slay your father, time will slay him, that is a virtual certainty." A son's task lies elsewhere: "to reproduce every one of the enormities touched upon in this manual, but in attenuated form. You must become your father, but a paler, weaker version of him" (DF, p. 145). "Patricide" is the last of the twenty-three subchapters, and anticipates not only the novel's end but its imagined aftermath, which is an eternally regenerated loop in which Thomas will adopt all of the Dead Father's qualities displayed in the initial chapters and eventually be hauled to his grave himself.

Barthelme thus uses commentary not as a reflection of the novel's action but as a device to make that action all the more integral. His central character only has to *be* in order for the narrrative to get under way and take shape. Much of what the father does is described by the part of speech known as the gerund, the form a verb takes when functioning as a noun. It is appropriate to the Dead Father's presence in the novel because it is his action that serves as a subject. When denied sex, he "slips his cable" and sets off on an orgy of "slaying." A page-long catalog of slayed objects follows, beginning with such odd things as "a grove of music and musicians," including "a harpist and then a performer upon the serpent and also a banger upon the rattle," and then "two virtuosos of the quail whistle and a zampogna player whose fingering of the chanters was sweet to the ear and by-the-bye and during a rest period he slew four buzzers and a shawmist and one blower upon the water jar" (DF, p. 11), the catalog soon running into a virtuoso display of language, which is after all what the Dead Father hopes to achieve. "My anger" (DF, p. 12), he says proudly as the dust settles, its demonstration being a matter for words as much as deeds. In a parallel way his attempted seduction of Julie is mounted with further doings, again basically linguistic, as he recounts his long list of "fatherings." It is once more a page-long catalog, which begins, "I fathered upon her in those nights the poker chip, the cash register, the juice extractor, and kazoo, the rubber pretzel, the cuckoo clock, the key chain . . ." (DF, p. 36). As with Barthelme's lists and litanies from his earlier short stories, this display invites a virtuosity of poetic sound and associative nonsense, all of which is justified by the narrative occasion. It is another example of language being its own subject rather than referring to something else, and here serves the purposes of a logically consecutive tale of considerable length. Given the story at hand, the father can break into this behavior at the slightest provocation, such as when his speech in chapter 7 is dismissed as the maunderings of "an old fart" (DF, p. 52). Appropriately, the son's reaction to such doings is in linguistic kind, a prolonged contemplation of "murderinging" (DF, p. 46), the proper form for a word denoting not an expressed action but a feeling Thomas wishes to nurse and savor.

The narrative goes on so long—long enough for a respectable novel—because of something else inherent in the Dead Father's being: a dogged persistence, making "stumbling from the stage . . . anathema to them . . . they want to be nuzzling new women when they are ninety" (DF, p. 78). These comments from Julie identify another theme, the Dead Father's insistence on monopolizing sexual attention. Her and Emma's resistance and Thomas's attempts to cut him out of the action prompt the rages of slaying, but there is also room for debate: the women's emerging feminism, characterized as a contrast of generations as well as gender, and providing a series of conflicts that complicate the progress to the grave and enlarge the scope of narrative. Consider how the Dead Father's tale of fatherings, intended as a vehicle of seduction, draws an entirely different reaction from the young women:

> Infuckingcredible, said Julie.
>
> Unfuckingbelievable, said Emma.
>
> Rudolf Rassendyll himself could not have managed the affair better.
>
> Yes, the Dead Father said, and on that bank of the river there stands to this day a Savings & Loan Association. A thing I fathered.
>
> Forfuckingmidable, said Julie. I suddenly feel all mops and brooms.
>
> Refuckingdoubtable, said Emma. I suddenly feel a saint of the saucepan.
>
> Six and three quarters percent compounded momentarily, said the Dead Father. I guarantee it.
>
> A bumaree, said Julie, they have this way of having you feel tiny and small.
>
> They are good at it, said Emma.
>
> We are only tidderly-push to the likes of them.
>
> See themselves as a rope to the eye of a needle, said Emma. (DF, p. 38)

The women's slang marks them of a different age, but even more so their new perspective on the relationship of women and men suggests another adversarial theme in the narrative's progress, that "but for a twist of fate we and not they would be calling the tune" (DF, p. 39). In time specific conflicts will arise, such as with a strange tribe known as the Wends, who avoid the whole problem by never taking wives but only having mothers, thus fathering themselves. There is the "Manual for Sons"'s concluding hope that fatherhood, if not something that can be overcome, may at least be turned down. Feminism, then, is as much a counterforce to Dead Fatherhood as anything a son might construe—and is, as we shall see, more effective in establishing itself as an alternative.

The most immediate alternative, however, is that of language itself: especially language in dimensions other than the linear. The inexorable nature of Dead Fatherhood finds its structural complement in the novel's linear progress; hauling the old man to his grave is necessary because of who he is, and it takes so long because of how he acts. Both qualities bear directly on the thematic problem Barthelme's novel wishes to debate. The terms of that debate are structured as variations on, digressions from, or conflicts with that linear progress. The narrative rhythm is established as a series of forward starts interrupted by various pauses and disruptions, and in nearly all cases these variations from the line forward take the shape of language loosened from its strictly narrative duty.

The first example is rudimentary in its simplicity, a practice Barthelme follows from his short stories, which often take such steps when introducing readers to a new technique. It happens during the first rest break, when the crew takes leave for lunch and the principals settle down around a picnic cloth for food and conversation. Here the author looks back to *City Life* for two spatialized techniques to emphasize the shift from linear narrative: a boxlike diagram set at the top of the page (with Thomas, Julie, and the Dead Father occupying three sides, and the prawns they are dining on set on the fourth), plus a column of unpunctuated, unmodified dialogue that constitutes their table talk:

> Quite good.
> Not so bad.
> Is there mustard?
> In the pot.
> Something in it.
> What?
> Look there.
> Pick it out with your finger.
> Nasty little bugger.
> Pass the prawns.
> And for dessert?
> Fig Newtons. (DF, p. 8)

Both form and subject depart from the narrative, as if making a statement that words can be used another way and that there is more to life (and to Barthelme's novel) than just trudging forward. What the content of the talk adds isn't nothing, but rather a statement of how the idea of "nothing" is always a possibility no matter how inexorable the marching onward may seem. It is a momentary opening in the narrative's otherwise strictly progressive form, and—early as it comes—sets the terms for subsequent interruptions, most of which will be more structurally and thematically serious.

The table talk dialogue is a cue to Barthelme's more complex technique (anticipating several of the stories in Great Days [1979]), which will float such free-standing lines quite apart from either narrative or internal sequence. The first of four such sections stretches from page 23 to 27 (the others are on pp. 60–64, 85–90, and 147–55), and consists of apparent mishmash such as:

> Whose little girl are you?
> I get by, I get by.
> Time to go.
> Hoping this will reach you at a favorable moment.
> Bad things can happen to people.
> Is that a threat?
> Dragged him all this distance without any rootytoottoot.
> Is that a threat? (DF, p. 23)

Snatches of continuity never last more than a line or two, and most statements are disembodied phrases, such as the fourth, which is repeated several times in the section along with other such dangling notions. What happens is that, freed from linear necessity, other structural combinations take form, spatially and as play. Clichés bounce off implied messages while still other ideas come rolling in at random; yet by virtue of their proximity to these other lines, they help form a constellation of meaning all their own.

The purpose these self-consciously fragmentary sections serve in the novel's larger narrative plan becomes evident by considering their context—in particular, by what prompts them. The first occurs in chapter 3, after Thomas, Emma, and Julie view a pornographic movie. The film is described at some length, its subject and action recountable as a series of structural combinations beginning with a one-on-one encounter that grows through various permutations into full-fledged group sex, ending with a panoply of viewing opportunities both on the screen and among the audience ("Some members of the group watching screen, some watching Emma, some watching Emma / screen / Emma / screen, some watching Emma / screen / Julie / screen / Thomas" [DF, p. 22]). The randomly combinatory nature of the dialogue lines, then, are prepared for by the similar style of sex on screen and the possible perspectives in viewing it. Next time around it is the hauling crew's discontent in chapter 8 that sparks some complaints from the women, which turn into several pages of rebounding lines; then the unease caused by a following horseman in chapter 13 precedes a similar resumption, until chapter 18 can stand alone as the fourth example. Consisting of lines just from Julie and Emma, most of which are identifiable as comments from the woman's point of view, it needs no other prompting than the novel's general movement away from the masculine toward the feminine, indicating that for Barthelme the nature of these dialogue sessions—loosely presented, with almost no linear organization, yet inviting new spatial associations—is womanly, at the farthest remove possible from the ethos of the Dead Father.

Other examples of language coming to the fore enhance this notion of the feminine as a counterforce (and successor) to Dead Fatherhood. In chapter 7 the Dead Father is allowed to make a speech, something he's been requesting to do since being relieved of his belt buckle by Thomas. That the roots of this speech are in obfuscation is clear from the brief debate that precedes it—the father insisting he has given Thomas his buckle, the son reminding him that no, it has been taken away from him. When his speech begins, it is at once an example of pure language. But not the sharply material exchanges of Julie and Emma. Instead, the Dead Father rambles on in a muddle of disembodied connectives and random qualifiers: "In considering, he said, inconsidering inconsidering inconsidering the additionally arriving human beings annually additionally arriving human beings each producing upon its head one hundred thousand individual hairs some retained and some discarded . . ." (DF, pp. 49–50). Boring from its first phrase, it is too tedious for even the other men, who sit down and begin chatting among themselves. Yet the Dead Father drones on for another page and a half, his blathering giving not a clue to his listeners until he pauses significantly for applause. With none of the catchy rhythms and delightfully new associations of the women's talk, which has its own life and lively personality and sparks the reader's interest by virtue of its fresh attention to the world, the Dead Father's speech establishes nothing except his Dead Fatherhood, a reminder that simply having language *be* rather than *be about* is no guarantee in itself of value. Rather it is a shorthand manner of reestablishing the character's identity and demand for authority. Yet that manner is not short enough for his listeners, nor as concise as his son's ability to save time and space, as when during a conversation with Julie, whose lines are sharply to the point, "Thomas spoke a long paragraph to the effect that [the point at hand] was true" (DF, p. 69).

Male speech in *The Dead Father*, while never uninteresting, is almost always shaped by clichés and delivered with an unmerited stylistic flamboyance that has the reader wishing for these figures to be taken from the stage—which is precisely what Dead Fatherhood resists. Even the hauling crew, who hardly ever speak, cannot do so without falling into stereotypical poses; their list of grievances delivered in chapter 14 is concocted in a style of cowpoke lingo, labor movement rhetoric, and philosophical inquiry, all run together in a way that sacrifices meaning to stock effect. Then there are the apes, particularly Julie's dance partner, whose natural inability to carry on a conversation suggests all the times she's been crucified on her own lines of dialogue when trying to talk with men:

> Can you talk at all?
> (Silence.)
> Nothing?
> (Silence.)
> That's new.
> (Silence.)
> You apes live around here in the dense underbrush and move in and out among the trees seeking fruits and vegetables?
> (Silence.)
> Well you certainly are accomplished dancers except perhaps maybe you're holding me a little tight?
> (Silence.) (DF, p. 101)

The "Manual for Sons" catalogs male language from the epic tongue-lashing to the typical fumblings of fatherly talks. In this section Barthelme shows how Dead Fathers everywhere establish their identity with language, such as "Hey son. Hey boy. Let's you and me go out and throw the ball around. Throw the ball around. You don't want to go out and throw the ball around? How come you don't want to go out and throw the ball around?" and "You want to hep me work on the patio? Sure you do. Sure you do. We gonna have us a fine-lookin' patio there boy. . . . C'mon kid, I'll let you hold the level. And this time I want you to hold the fucking thing straight" (DF, p. 125). Finally, the novel itself grants the Dead Father a chapter of last words, before the closing section bulldozes him into the grave. Appropriately to Barthelme's aesthetic, these words in chapter 22 are Joycean, a language salad in the manner of *Finnegans Wake*, that last gasp of modernism reaching toward but not grasping the new order of the postmodern.

That order must await the larger construct of *The Dead Father*, a structure more involved than the simple unleashing of words along the lines of chapter 22's "AndI. EndI. Great endifarce teeterteeterteetertottering. Willit urt. I reiterate. Don't be cenacle. Conscientia mille testes" (DF, p. 171). The last chapter takes the Dead Father, whose rant and bluster have sustained him (if not the postmodern reader) in the face of earlier slights and challenges, and forces him to deal with the succeeding generation on its own terms, in this case tight lines of dialogue resulting from his desire to "touch the golden fleece" (Julie's pudendum):

> After all this long and arduous and if I may say so rather ill-managed journey? Not to touch it? What am I to do?
>   You are to get into the hole, said Thomas.
>   Get into the hole?
>   Lie down in the hole.
>   And then you'll cover me up?
>   The bulldozers are just over the hill, Thomas said, waiting.
>   You'll bury me alive?
>   You're not alive, Thomas said, remember? (DF, p. 175)

These clipped lines are not, however, the final word. Rather, as with the unfettered play of the women's conversations and the apt analyses of the "Manual for Sons," Barthelme's novel frees language from no-longer-valid constraining principles and lets it construe something new. It becomes the women's task rather than the son's; the fate of Thomas, after all, is to go on fathering, impregnating the world with the material issue of his own ideas, whereas Julie and Emma have shown that they can use language for purposes beyond reference.

Like certain of Barthelme's early stories, parts of The Dead Father struggle with the notion of text in search of just such freedom. That struggle, however, is always a male affair, such as the Dead Father's business with collecting and comparing editions in chapter 2 (replete with the arcane language of bibliographers and bookmen) and the son's story (filling chapter 6) about battling a serpent for the indistinguishable text held in its mouth. In terms of Dead Fatherhood per se, the climactic text is discussed and written in chapter 20, where the old man reluctantly drafts his will, a disorganized list of objects that reflect on his life of male dominance. Unlike the women's language, there is no hidden genius to these words; they are simply fragments of a life style that's no longer a valid option for the world Thomas and Julie and Emma will inherit.

Instead, the novel has been taking shape for the expression of new linguistic truths, truths which acknowledge that fatherly intentionality alone does not create existence, but that the generative power of language's own system must be taken into account—something the women rather than the men have been doing. It is, after all, systematics that defeat the Dead Father more than anything else, and it has been the women's play with language that brings that sense of system to the fore. The novel itself has adapted itself to this understanding, allowing for graphic shapes (the square picnic cloth for lunch, the line of march, the circle that Julie devises as a new seating plan for meals) and a continual series of litanies, catalogs, and inventories, ending with mother's grocery list in chapter 21, ironically the most important for sustaining life.

But what the defamiliarized language, pointing to structures rather than sense, accomplishes is to open an understanding which emotions block off. Barthelme's writing has allowed readers to see through the Dead Father's bluster and the son's ambivalence, and to appreciate how the women's creative play with language yields new artifacts pleasing in themselves and also expressive of a more satisfactory relation with the world, a world fathers would dominate to destruction and sons might fumble with to exasperation. The extent of this novel's linguistic liberation is that it even makes sentimental language once more possible. Where in other circumstances the reader might well turn away from such suspected manipulation, the narrative form of The Dead Father earns the right to present sentimentality in its clear state as system—as a construct with all its artifice apparent and working parts on display, yet humanly effective nevertheless.

The key passage comes near the end of "A Manual for Sons," which after many examples of fatherly behavior shifts focus for a moment to the distance a son may feel and how that distancing puzzles the father. At this point the text explains, in phrases that advance tentatively, halt for reexamination, then venture forth with a cautious explanation to the old man of why his son bears such anger:

> He is mad about being small when you were big, but no, that's not it, he is mad about being helpless when you were powerful, but no, not that either, he is mad about being contingent when you were necessary, not quite it, he is insane because when he loved you, you didn't notice. (DF, p. 143)

With The Dead Father published, Donald Barthelme finds himself precisely at midcareer. A novel each from the decade preceding and succeeding frame it; there have been five short story collections before, and five more will follow; the thin, oversize delight of his children's book, The Slightly Irregular Fire Engine (1971), finds its complement in his similar-sized volume for twisted young adults done with cartoonist Seymour Chwast, Sam's Bar: An American Landscape (1987); and tragically, time will allow just fourteen more years to exactly complement his first fourteen as a published fiction writer before he dies at age fifty-eight, having just completed a work of pleasantly relaxed play, the illustrated and allegorical historical romance titled The King (1990).

How Barthelme's fiction develops from 1975 onward is a less dramatic story than that of the literary disruptions and radically new formations evident in his work from 1961 to The Dead Father. There is, in fact, a recreational tone to it, as if with the great obstacle of decayed modernism out of the way and the structural challenges of devising something new in its wake successfully met, the author can now take time to work among the great range of readerly delights his writing has made possible. It is significant that he titles his third novel *Paradise* (1986), for the work is a comically indulgent exercise in notions of just what a thematic and structural paradise might be, proposed as they are in Barthelme's customary tone of whimsical self-criticism. The location is retrieved from *Snow White*: a large, mostly bare apartment in Greenwich Village, once more in terms with the region's times, which have now moved beyond sexual revolution to a more considered examination of women's enfranchisement in sex, language, and authority. The situation takes advantage of *The Dead Father*'s themes and techniques, as a male protagonist both enjoys the attentions of three young women who move in and suffers their reexamination of his ethics and aesthetics. About the same length as the first two novels, *Paradise* uses their short forms as well, breaking the narrative into many small sections that shift time and space as if these entities are merely narrative episodes on the track of some greater interest.

There are also ways that *Paradise* reaches beyond Barthelme's first two novels. Instead of *The Dead Father*'s unity of action, this new work builds upon a unity of place—to the protagonist's apartment and otherwise predictable life within, these three young women bring new and strange ideas and practices, including a different language that disrupts the syntax he has used so well thus far. His locale, in fact, becomes a focus for intrusions of all sorts, including street noise, new styles of sex, and texts such as he's never before read. All of these influences intrude as alien forces, but by reshaping the novel's own texture become, by its end, the new cultural definition of reality (something *The Dead Father* suggests but does not itself achieve).

Barthelme takes the trouble to signal how his third novel has something new in mind. It isn't like his first: he asks halfway through, at the same point where *Snow White*'s ongoing narrative had paused for the reader to answer a questionnaire about the story and its form, "What if they all lived happily ever after together?" but decides at once that such is "an unlikely prospect" (P, p. 100). A bit later Simon, his protagonist, does some reexamining when his father dies, but rejects the second novel's plan as well: "The death of the father is supposed to release a burst of new creative energy, he remembered. He felt nothing but sadness and admiration"

(P, p. 139). And so Barthelme's character is left to face the situation without the options *Snow White* and *The Dead Father* would provide. Unlike *The King, Paradise* is no allegorical reprise, but rather a genuine (if smaller) step forward in the author's development as a novelist.

Like any conventional novel, Barthelme's third finds reason to begin with a change in life: his hero, a middle-aged man named Simon, has rented a new, mostly bare apartment following his separation, and is just moving in. But not alone—that is the first disruption, and quite a surprising one. Three young women are coming with him, models he has just met in a bar where they show lingerie (and themselves) to the male patrons at cocktail hour. The reason they need a place to live is even more surprising. They've made a financial miscalculation, cutting things too close, not for any normal budgetary reason but because of charity. "The hell of it is, we gave all this money to Africa," one of them—Dore—complains. "That's why we're so low. We each sent three thousand bucks to Africa. To alleviate hunger. We saw this thing on television" (P, p. 13). All Simon had originally bargained for was "a sabbatical," taking leave of both home and business in another town ostensibly to avoid the death threats of an angry contractor he's faulted, but mostly because he can't bear "the prospect of listening to his wife's voice for another hour, another minute" (P, p. 35). Now, however, he must attend to the radically new voices of Dore, Veronica, and Anne—not just creatures of a different sex but of a whole new age and world. Although in a new city and new apartment, almost bare to the walls, Simon has brought his attitudes, not even recognizing them as such but assuming that by long usage his way of dealing with life is the natural way, the only way. From the moment he meets these three, his nicely ordered world view begins to deconstruct, and that deconstruction forms the narrative action of *Paradise*.

"Q: You're how tall?" "A: Six foot and a bit." "Q: Not much hair." "Lucky to have what I've got" (P, p. 14). With this interrogation the novel's alternating rhythm of action and examination begins. Simon will be questioned periodically on how his life with the girls developed, and the manner of these talks—starting with such specifics as height, weight, and general health—is posed as a phenomenology, assuming nothing and asking Simon to describe his new experience as he might to a visitor from another planet. And what the young women are revealing to him at times seems like just that, an entire level of behavior he has previously just glimpsed from afar if at all. Nevertheless the method lets him detail this world with a fidelity equal to Balzacian mannerism, something the postmodern novel would not on its own terms allow and had therefore remained beyond the scope of *Snow White* and *The Dead Father*:

> Q: Did they just hang around all day, or what?
>
> A: They came and went. They enjoyed the city. They went to Bloomingdale's and the Met. They went to the Cloisters. They went to Asti's and banged on their water glasses while the Anvil Chorus was being sung. They went to Sweet Basil and heard Wynton Marsalis. I went with them that night, he played very well, had his brother Branford on tenor. They went to the Museum of Modern Art and bought postcards in the gift shop. They went to Lincoln Center and saw various things, the film festival and all that. They got excited by the Strand and came back with books. They went to the Palladium and saw Lily Tomlin or somebody. They didn't always go together. Sometimes Veronica and Dore went, sometimes Anne went by herself, and so on. Sometimes they went together to Balducci's and came home with various exotic foods. They cooked together, sometimes. I remember a particularly good Cream of Four Onion soup. They spent a lot of time just walking around and looking at things. I think they were happy. Although in limbo. (P, p. 28)

Mannerist in detail, the paragraph's effect remains postmodern thanks to Barthelme's ability to weave these elements as a texture of signs rather than just references. The selection of items is a good one, comprising the high points of a lively young woman's life in Manhattan of the mid-1980s. But the passage is not just a notebook record, for like the women hopping from trendy place to place, the sentences themselves rarely pause for any studied effect, excepting only where Simon has been touched (the jazz group's good performance, the delicious onion soup). For Dore, Veronica, and Anne themselves, the world is just a whirling presence, its fine points indistinguishable from its rush of action. What did they shop for at Bloomie's? We're never told, and they themselves might not know—

they were just shopping, an activity with no specific errand in mind but just an exercise of its own being. In "The New Music," a story collected in *Great Days* (1979), the author had written a paean to this life style, itself a question-and-answer description of a man who sets out one morning to go xeroxing, sees a young woman whose glance is smoldering, and is told she's just practicing. Like the gerunds in *The Dead Father*, these are examples of subjects that define themselves by their being. And here in *Paradise* those definitions provide a manneristic portrait of the current world that would otherwise be technically impossible.

Because much of what the young women do is legible to Simon only on the level of sign—the physical incarnation of a referential device rather than a conceptual journey to what the representation is or means—a great deal of *Paradise* is spent putting those signs in play, where they can associate by themselves rather than as indications of something else. The three of them sport words with no meanings: "Breasts waver and dip and sway from side to side under t-shirts with messages so much of the moment that Simon doesn't understand a tenth of them: ALLY SHEEDY LIVES! Who is Ally Sheedy? In what sense does she live, and why is the fact worthy of comment? They know, he doesn't." More accurately, he *assumes* they know. But when their next shirt boasts a visage of Pierre Trudeau and Simon re-calls that he has actually met this personage at a planning conference "and found him a charming and thoughtful man," the girls don't care. "This earns him about a crayon's worth of credit with his guests" (P, p. 43). Their politics are no more logically consequential, derived as they are "from a K-Mart of sources, Thomas Aquinas marching shoulder-to-shoulder with Simone de Beauvoir and the weatherbeaten troopers of *Sixty Minutes*. They were often to the left and right during the same conversation, sometimes the same sentence" (P, p. 133). Yet such appraisals, and the very notions of left and right, are Simon's own—relics of his system of belief that may not fit theirs at all and ignores the fact that when it comes to t-shirts and politics the three young women don't have a system at all, just a card deck of signs that are fashionable not for what they signify but for what they are in themselves; a shirt's meaning, after all, is as a piece of clothing, and only in that sense, and not as a coherent political theorem, does it signify.

Simon does appreciate that his guests speak a private language, and recalls that he and his wife spoke one too. But theirs was a grammar of irony, functioning as barbed little comments against the linguistic system that by virtue of orientation stayed within it. Such notions come out during Simon's interrogations, as when he characterizes his special interest, his spare-time activity as adultery and his wife's greatest want as "more fun" (P, p. 20). The wife herself is recalled as a master of such forms, notably the confession "I love you but it's only temporary" and her sentiment conveyed at weddings, "Here's wishing you a happy and successful first marriage" (P, p. 109). The two languages do touch when Dore, Veronica, and Anne discuss the sex they are sharing with him, and here the interfacing of systems gets painfully personal. In his absence they discuss Simon's excess age and weight and lagging stamina; true, they've seen porno films where even more women are serviced, but that's by "special guys" (P, p. 49). They consider lubricants and stimulants. In bed with him, they come up with the most unintentionally devastating lines: "Have you ever done this before?" and "Is this a male fantasy for you?" (P, pp. 54–55). The finest narrative effects come when the systems themselves collide, as he tries to interpret their words and drifts back into the routines of his own:

> "You're not a father-figure. That surprise you?"
> "No."
> "You're more like a guy who's stayed out in the rain too long."
> Does this translate into *experienced, tried-and-true, well-tempered*? Or *pulpy, hanging-in-thin-strips*? He pulls at an ear.
> "I mean worn, but with a certain character."
> Rust never sleeps, he thinks. "Well," he says, "shall we take the children to school?"
> "What children?"
> "Right." (P, pp. 112–13)

The sex they share is happy and rewarding for all four of them. The problems in their relationship run deeper, to language but also to how its different uses tend to alienate. The girls are a tribe unto themselves, and from Simon's perspective look just as wanting as his initially unspectacular sexuality had seemed to them. They aren't dumb, but "what they knew was so wildly various, a ragout of Spinoza and Cyndi Lauper with a William

Buckley sherbet floating in the middle of it" (P, p. 59). He demands imperiously that they at least know their own history, but his personal pride in having mastered existence is countered by their innocent observation that "I guess you old guys know a lot of different stuff, don't you?" (P, p. 61), his knowledge being just as much of a random ragout to anyone not specially cued in. He is not necessarily better or smarter, just twice as old. When their happiness starts to crumble, it is because their worlds (and not their sex) are out of touch:

> "You don't care about anything, Simon. You just go along cooking dinner and fucking us indiscriminately and reading The Wall Street Journal. Your vital interests are not involved here. You don't give a shit."
> (P, p. 162)

In the meantime the women have been reading feminist texts, but the ones that make their case the best are those that Simon reads as a habit of his being, trying to defend himself against the charge of considering them "dumb bunnies" as he stands there holding his copy of Audubon Action open to "Arizona Dam Project Faces New Challenge" (P, p. 187).

Most of all, Dore, Veronica, and Anne want Simon to treat them "as individuals" (P, p. 105), but that is just what the narrative situation will not let him do. The story's energy derives from there being three of them, its narrative sparked by the unusualness (and of course salaciousness) of not just one young woman moving in, but three. In basest terms, it is what prompts the reader to read this tale, but on a structural level it is what generates Barthelme's telling as well. Because there are three and not one, everything becomes different, from the configurations of sex (which attract interest) to the different ways every daily activity, from shopping and eating to relaxing and sleeping, has to be managed. Simon's perspective sets the parameters within which all this begins to happen; but as the action takes place, it systematically eludes those limits as the generational and gender-based distinctions between the protagonist and his guests assert themselves.

Paradise is therefore a narrative fated to deconstruct itself. If *Snow White* builds itself upon stasis (the fairy tale characters unable to follow the Grimms-Disney script while puzzling over their states of being) and *The*

Dead Father exercises itself along a clear and active line of progress, *Paradise* forms itself as dissolution. As with the best of Donald Barthelme's work, it is a lesson in postmodernism, for what begins as an ideal narrative situation (from the basest point of view, that of male sexual fantasy, the most selfish form of story making) establishes itself as a narrative unmaking. From the most conventionally promising of circumstances, the novel virtually erases itself in terms of possibility, until at the end Simon is left with nothing but a dangling conversation with the book's interrogator, filling empty time pleasantly enough as did the women in *The Dead Father*. Only now the women are no longer there.

Chapter Five

Later Fiction

The second half of Donald Barthelme's canon, accomplished in the fourteen years following publication of *The Dead Father*, sounds a different note in the tonality of his short fiction. The stories are more relaxed and more generously entertaining, with as many comic effects as the earlier pieces but now with the humor not at the expense of an older tradition but drawn from the properties of Barthelme's own style. No longer will Kafka or Tolstoy be asked to sit uncomfortably within the outrageously inappropriate confines of our postmodern world; instead, the author's confidence with that world will let him joke with it on its own terms. Nor will there be a cubist disorder of conversations at birthday parties or cinema vérité pieces that steadfastly refuse to cohere. There will be precious few fragments, for now Barthelme has more trust in his ability to comprehend an overall situation—and most of all trust that his readers will not make more of them than he intends, the fear of which had kept his earlier short stories so defiantly anti-illusionistic.

With *Amateurs* (1976) the feeling is most immediately one of comfort, both of Barthelme in his role of writer and the readers in their roles as consumers of his stories. The opening piece, "Our Work and Why We Do It," refers to Barthelme's frequently expressed opinion that he could be quite happy back in his previous job of assembling, composing, and laying out the contents of a magazine as its managing editor. The narrator is supervising a press, up to his elbows in "problems of makeready, registration, showthrough, and feed" (*A*, p. 4). But just as these unfamiliar terms have easy, functional meanings (once learned), so too are there equally mechanical solutions. No endless debates between Kierkegaard and Schlegel, no hapless protagonists pondering their existential fates—just the artistic pleasure of putting machines to work at producing the most wonderful things:

> The tiny matchbook-cover press is readied, the packing applied, the "Le Foie de Veau" form locked into place. We all stand around a small table watching the matchbook press at work. It is exactly like a toy steam engine. Everyone is very fond of it, although we also have a press big as a destroyer escort—that one has a crew of thirty-five, its own galley, its own sick bay, its own band. We print the currency of Colombia, and the Acts of the Apostles, and the laws of the land, and the fingerprints. (*A*, p. 5)

Within this happy context, Barthelme is able to play at language and idea with all the verve of his earlier fiction. The situation prompts a simile, and one simile prompts another, which is all it takes to turn loose his talents of linguistic invention. True, presses are run by a crew, just like navy ships—so why not add the other things navy ships have? As for what they print, the items seem extravagantly odd and random—except that all four exist in this world as printed objects and therefore have to be printed somewhere. Because these workers are pressmen and not writers, they are under no obligation to make the subjects cohere. They just print them, and are therefore granted a rare pleasure of play and association—the same pleasures Barthelme gives his reader in this narrative.

Within this story that typifies *Amateurs* are most of Barthelme's familiar techniques. Skinny lists of terms, here the names of typefaces, run down the page in one of the author's favorite forms, the litany. Other texts literally crash through the windows, bringing the same excitement as do the salesmen, rushing through the doors with new orders. The one element missing is that of graphic collage. But the press functions and typeface features take that role, and the story's busy tone is reminiscent of Barthelme's collage story from *Sadness*, "The Flight of Pigeons from the Palace." In that piece, however, the narrator had been driven nearly to exhaustion by having to come up with marvel after new marvel to delight audiences. Here there is no such worry, because the work is invigorating, rewarding, and unlikely to dissipate in either exhaustion or obsolescence. "Our reputation for excellence is unexcelled, in every part of the world," Barthelme's narrator concludes. "And will be maintained until the destruction of our art by some other art which is just as good but which, I am happy to say, has not yet been invented" (A, p. 9).

Such is the condition in which Donald Barthelme finds his own work as the 1970s end. After a decade and a half of innovation, perforce disruptive because of the modernist traditions and conventions that stood in his way, and after the equally taxing struggle to establish his own postmodern mastery of the novel, he could—much like this story's pressman—settle more comfortably into a style of fiction writing that he knew would remain the standard of both excellence and currency for some time. Although the heyday of innovative fiction's spectacular accomplishments was over, it was now established as the mainstream—sufficiently mainstream for it to be attacked as Barthelme and his generation had challenged fiction a decade and a half before. And for the time being these challenges had been met. The attempts of John Gardner's On Moral Fiction (1978) and Gerald Graff's Literature against Itself (1979) to roll back standards to those of moralism and modernism had been resisted, and the next style of fiction, the Minimalism espoused by Raymond Carver, Ann Beattie, and younger brother Frederick Barthelme, had emerged by drawing as much on innovative fiction's imaginative freedom as on realism's figuration. The answer had been play: not the cocky, disruptive, irreverent play that subverted modernism in Come Back, Dr. Caligari, but a more harmlessly engaging style of amusement that takes the givens of both moralism and realism and good naturedly stands them on their heads.

In Amateurs Barthelme finds occasion for such overturnings in "The School," whose life-or-death issue is the 100 percent mortality rate suffered by the pets and projects of a grade school class (starting with its tree plantings, continuing with its gerbil, and reaching the apex of anxiety with the demise of its sponsored third-world orphan), and in "Porcupines at the University," an earlier story passed over several times before but now updated and added to the canon as a way of showing how the most unlikely and mutually alien subjects can be melded into a coherent story if all are treated strictly in character with the tools of literary realism (the situation involves a herd of porcupines being driven by porcupine wranglers across a college campus beleaguered by its own problems of disruption and dissent). In Great Days (1979) Barthelme shifts from subject and theme to structure and formal technique, yet keeps the same ideals of comedy and play in mind by focusing on the performative—a stylistic equivalent of the activities represented in *Amateurs* (class projects expiring, porcupines being wrangled, presses being run). Together, these collections reveal a confidence with subject and form equal to almost any previous high point in the development of the American short story.

Not surprisingly, this emphasis on performance coincides with the use of that most performative of American art forms, jazz, as a topic for several stories collected in *Great Days*. After "The Crisis" has begun the volume with a cautiously restrained examination of texture and surface and "The Apology" has moved more obviously into a jazz idiom by showing how an overwilling apologizer can drive away an offended suitor with a rifflike assemblage of overstated regrets, Barthelme offers a piece whose title tells the reader just what these words are meant to create: "The New Music," in which standards of musical composition enhance the systematics of linguistics that the author has used before to expand the dimensions of narrative.

In both music and speech, rhythms are carriers of meaning. Rhythmic dialogues make statements far beyond the content of conceptual exchange; consider how the structure of something as simple as "Where did you go? Out. What did you do? Nothing" says so much that it becomes the title of a humorous commentary on childhood's disaffections. In Barthelme's "The New Music," the entire story is constituted of just such a disconnected dialogue, a mode he introduces here and continues in several other pieces as the collection's most distinguishing form. Canonically, it is the style of talk Julie and Emma exchanged in *The Dead Father* as a way of generating a new linguistic reality far beyond the constraints of both the father's and son's self-serving forms. Now in *Great Days* story after story can be produced by its creative possibilities, with a confidence detached from narrative explanations and contextual justifications. What the characters do in "The New Music" is rarely directed toward a goal or even an object, but rather expresses its own sense of activity:

—What did you do today?
—Went to the grocery store and Xeroxed a box of English muffins,

two pounds of ground veal and an apple. In flagrant violation of the
Copyright Act.

      . . . .

—Ah well. I was talking to a girl, talking to her mother actually
but the daughter was very much present, on the street. The daughter
was absolutely someone you'd like to take to bed and hug and kiss, if
you weren't too old. If she weren't too young. She was a wonderful-
looking young woman and she was looking at me quite seductively,
very seductively, smoldering a bit, and I was thinking quite well of myself, very well indeed, thinking myself quite the—Until I realized she
was just practicing. (GD, pp. 21–22)

The most frequent words in this passage, like the activities themselves, are
simple gerunds: ing words that, by virtue of their lacking an object, refer
simply to themselves. Placed in the context of unintroduced and unpunctuated dialogue, they have no reason for existence except their own play,
which Barthelme masters in a way both pleasing and amusing to his
readers. The effect is that of jazz improvisation, especially the style of two
instruments trading four-bar phrases back and forth in such a way that each
complements the other's action while still advancing its own, as happens
in a section of "The New Music," originally published in The New Yorker of
October 2, 1978, as "Momma":

    —Momma didn't 'low no clarinet playing in here. Unfortunately.
    —Momma.
    —Momma didn't 'low no clarinet playing in here. Made me sad.
    —Momma was outside.
    —Momma was very outside.
    —Sitting there, 'lowing and not-'lowing. In her old rocking chair.
    —'Lowing this, not-'lowing that.
    —Didn't 'low oboe.
    —Didn't 'low gitfiddle. Vibes.
    —Rock over your damn foot and bust it, you didn't pop to when
she was 'lowing and not-'lowing.
    —Right. 'Course, she had all the grease.
    —True.

—You wanted a little grease, like to buy a damn comic book or something, you had to go to Momma.

—Sometimes yes, sometimes no. Her variously colored moods.

—Mauve. Warm gold. Citizen's blue.

—Mauve mood that got her thrown in the jug that time. (GD, p. 29)

The European style of punctuating lines of dialogue makes them hang on the page, while their responsive rhythm creates a mood all its own: of reminiscing, another gerund that is even more convincing than the activities reported earlier, for now that activity is actually taking place.

Jazz provides a model for interacting rhythms, and is by nature an activity that represents nothing other than itself—postmodernism's own ideal for fictive writing. Even as a subject, it lets Barthelme take his narrative language further than other topics might always allow, as happens in a complementary story from *Great Days*, "The King of Jazz." The title is referential—to the 1930 movie featuring Paul Whiteman and his orchestra—but also reflective of practices in and around jazz, including the occasion of "cutting sessions" (where players compete against each other in jam sessions) and the way critics like to assign labels (making the title ironic, for Whiteman's popularized music made him anything but an innovator or key figure).

"Well I'm the king of jazz now, thought Hokie Mokie to himself as he oiled the slide on his trombone," the story begins—like many postmodern stories, just where a conventional tale would end. To reassure himself of such status Hokie plays a few notes out the window, which starts a critical dialogue between two passers-by. Can you tell who is playing, "Can you distinguish our great homemade American jazz performers, each from the other?" "Used to could," the friend replies, anticipating Simon's own little riff in *Paradise* when he challenges himself to name ten influential drummers in the history of jazz. "Then who is playing?" Easy: "Sounds like Hokie Mokie to me. Those few but perfectly selected notes have the real epiphanic glow" (GD, p. 55), which is itself a snatch of the language generated so facilely by the first generation of jazz critics (nearly all of them afterhours professors from Columbia and Rutgers).

The story proceeds by letting this style of language generate itself, as the tropes of literary criticism and art commentary spin out endlessly in an attempt to capture the essence of Hokie Mokie's music—which is, of course, something that neither written words nor painted objects can approximate. It is when Hokie is challenged by a young Japanese musician that the king's truly great playing—and the critical listeners' most extravagant play of comparisons—begins:

> "You mean that sound that sounds like the cutting edge of life? That sounds like polar bears crossing the Arctic ice pans? That sounds like a herd of musk ox in full flight? That sounds like male walruses diving to the bottom of the sea? That sounds like fumaroles smoking on the slopes of Mt. Katmai? That sounds like the wild turkey walking through the deep, soft forest? That sounds like beavers chewing trees in an Appalachian marsh? That sounds like an oyster fungus growing on an aspen trunk? That sounds like a mule deer wandering a montane of the Sierra Nevada? That sounds like prairie dogs kissing? That sounds like manatees munching seaweed at Cape Sable? That sounds like coatimundis moving in packs across the face of Arkansas? That sounds like—?" (GD, p. 59)

This is not at all what Hokie sounds like, for words cannot be music, and the terms themselves, by virtue of their references, are contradictory (how can turkeys and beavers and polar bears all sound the same? They can't; but the speaker's language about them does!). The activity of such language does approximate the activity of Hokie playing jazz, and unleashing that verbal improvisation is what "The King of Jazz" lets Barthelme do.

His next collection both continues this special interest and confirms its supporting style in the canon. The volume is itself a gesture toward canon formation: a tall, closely printed book running 457 pages titled *Sixty Stories* (1981) that combines nine new short stories with another 51 (of a possible 120) from the earlier gatherings. Gone from the living record are such self-consciously difficult pieces as "Florence Green Is 81" and "Bone Bubbles"; also missing are the purposely flat narratives of "Edward and Pia" and "A Few Moments of Sleeping and Waking." In their place, Barthelme's emphasis falls on his earlier experiments with playful delight such as "Me and Miss Mandible" and "The Balloon," while admitting two previously noncanonical pieces from *Guilty Pleasures* as full-fledged stories (and not just parodies)—a third will appear six years later in the companion volume, *Forty Stories*, to round out the author's hundred. There is even "A Manual for Sons" from *The Dead Father*, a self-contained story that employs similarly ludic devices and is written with the same sense of comic confidence that became the dominant mode of *Amateurs* and *Great Days*. From the latter, *Sixty Stories* reprints "The Crisis," "The New Music," and "The King of Jazz," while the former collection is represented by "The School" and "Our Work and Why We Do It" in *Sixty Stories* and "Porcupines at the University" in *Forty Stories*.

What distinguishes any retrospective exhibition is not just selections from the past but the nature of new work being shown at the same time. The last decade of Donald Barthelme's life is dominated by these kinds of gatherings, with just one volume of previously uncollected stories in between: *Overnight to Many Distant Cities* (1983). But since both retrospectives add new material, his writer's development can still be traced even in these mature years of canon stabilization.

Of Barthelme's three books from the 1980s, *Sixty Stories* is the simplest and most direct in terms of growth, for rounding out its selections from the author's earlier collections are nine new stories. All were published between November 27, 1978, and January 26, 1981, in the wake of *Great Days* and before the gathering for *Overnight to Many Distant Cities* commenced. In length, number, historical proximity, and relative affinity and diversity, they are presented just like the samplings from other collections preceding them in *Sixty Stories*. Of the nine, five are dash-dialogue stories, while others relish the odd details that give *Great Days* its special flavor. One piece, "The Farewell," picks up where "On the Steps of the Conservatory" left off, while another—"Bishop"—introduces the character whose similar story inaugurates the *Overnight* volume. Throughout the nine runs a consistent interest in language—not so much for the semiotic fascinations evident in Barthelme's earliest fiction, but more for the way certain nuances, drawn from various parts of the contemporary culture, form attractive and intriguing voices that can play off each other in dialogue or establish themselves as identifiable texts within the greater narrative.

Such voices, both by themselves and in conversation, are played to the full in "The Emerald," *Sixty Stories'* most obvious contribution to the

Barthelme style. Like the most radically experimental fictions of earlier collections, it was not first published in The New Yorker, but rather appeared in Esquire, in the November 1979 issue (and again in 1980 as a forty-page limited edition book published by Sylvester and Orphanos in Los Angeles). It is easily Barthelme's longest short story, eclipsing even "A Manual for Sons," which is given such generic status here. Yet for all its length, "The Emerald" manages to move along very quickly thanks to its author's customary lightness of style and snappiness of juxtapositional transitions. The new element is a characterizational and appealingly vocal use of language, which is generated not by philosophers or advertising copywriters but by various people who sound like they come from the streets of Greenwich Village or the towns of East Texas (Barthelme's two principal residences) and who speak with the quaint angularity sure to catch the ear of such a creative artist. In the dialogue sections, oddly named characters (Tope, Sallywag, Wide Boy, Taptoe) rifle clichés back and forth (sure as shootin', right as rain) as they lay plans for stealing the emerald and cutting it up for profit. In sections of a more extended conversation, Moll—the emerald's mother—finds out as much about the interviewing journalist as the journalist finds out about Moll. The interview does reveal that the greatest threat to Moll's emerald comes from a witch hunter named Vandermaster, which sets the stage for a meeting between these two as the story's protagonist and principal antagonist. Their dialogue is the piece's most inventive one, he mixing Joycean word salad with redneck vernacular, she sounding like both a sorceress and a street-tough feminist. Yet even the subplot has its special humor, as the journalist and her subject are manipulated by an unscrupulous editor while the interview itself, undertaken as the stuff of prize winning journalism, often devolves into questions such as "do you have a chili recipe you'd care to share with the folks?" (SS, p. 413).

The nine new short fictions in Sixty Stories also indicate the step Barthelme would take in Overnight to Many Distant Cities, his 1983 volume that stands as the last gathering of previously uncollected work published during his lifetime. Though at first glance Overnight is one of his more radical experiments, its fascination with the tones and textures of language is evident in Sixty Stories' "Aria," a 1979 New Yorker piece that stands as the first of the author's extended monologues. As an exercise in language, it complements the dash-dialogue stories by posing the reader as the story's other conversationalist. Or, if one wishes to remain uninvolved (something few postmodern readers can do), it can be said that the text in "Aria" interrogates itself. But in combination with such stories as "Bishop," where the concerns of daily life are as common as they were in "Critique de la Vie Quotidienne," this new mode of writing is less like the impenetrability of "Bone Bubbles" and "Sentence" and much more like the tenor of the *Overnight* collection, where the same character (consistently named "Bishop") is featured in the first full story and whose presence, as an icon of the author's own life in this world, remains a constant source of language and generator of narrative action.

The innovative nature of *Overnight to Many Distant Cities* is announced on its table of contents, for instead of listing the customary fourteen to sixteen new short stories, it alternates the titles of a dozen such pieces with the initial words (followed by three dots) of much shorter items in between. This structural distinction carries into the book itself, where the full-length fictions are printed in roman type while the miniatures are set in italics. The writing is all Barthelme's, and most of it is even from *The New Yorker*, with the occasional piece from another venue accommodated quite naturally within this new format. But the range of these materials is quite impressive, stretching from the author's main-line short stories to his unsigned "Comment" pieces from *The New Yorker*'s front pages, together with stories from such places as *Harper's* and *New American Review* and a contribution that first appeared in an art gallery's catalog. In the past, "Comment" and catalog writings had been consigned to a separate volume, *Great Days*, and then began appearing in other collections as exceptions rather than the rule. But with *Overnight to Many Distant Cities* a structure is devised to integrate the author's signed and unsigned work.

The obvious precedent for structuring a short story collection in this manner is Ernest Hemingway's *In Our Time* (1925). For this work the accepted interpretation is that by interleaving his fifteen full-length stories with an equal number of short, italicized passages Hemingway was able to have the cultural shock of World War I permeate the otherwise domestic business of such fictions as "The Three Day Blow," "The End of Something," and the two parts of "Big Two-Hearted River." Turning to Barthelme's experiment over half a century later, one must ask if the postmodern writer is using his own italicized interleavings for transitions, as associations, or for other reflective purposes. Unlike Hemingway, Barthelme has no agenda: there is nothing in *Overnight to Many Distant Cities* to suggest that one orders and controls in the imaginative life (Hemingway's roman typeface stories) what cannot be controlled in life (*In Our Time's* italicized "chapters"); nor is there any hint that art is neat while the world's a mess. For Barthelme, the eminent postmodernist, life and art are sometimes identical, driven as the former is by the latter's organizing principles. It is the interplay between *Overnight's* full stories and brief interpolations that establishes this principle not just as a thematic reference or technical trick but as a creative force in Donald Barthelme's work.

Story after story in *Overnight to Many Distant Cities* features characters caught up in the world of textuality, struggling to read their way through a culture where signs can be of more substance than the reality they might be presumed to signify. In "Visitors," the familiar protagonist named Bishop encounters movies, commercials, labels from art history, and made-for-seduction recipes during the summer interval when his fifteen-year-old daughter visits him. From this textual mélange he extracts a recipe for curing her persistent stomach ache—not a menu item, but a snappy chalk talk on the transition from Impressionism to Modernism. In "Affection" a married couple close to estrangement consult various textual sources for advice, from mother to fortune teller (Madam Olympia) and blues pianist (Sweet Pappa Cream Puff), all of whom contribute to the couple's eventual intertext, which is survived only thanks to the husband's increased earnings and his ability to not only read the *New York Times* but "wash it off my hands when I have finished reading it, every day" (*O*, p. 36). This theme continues through the volume, as Barthelme complements these recent stories with older material that had sat uncollected since 1971, such as "The Mothball Fleet" (where, in his more familiar manner of taking a metaphor and fleshing it out ad absurdum, the navy's flotilla of mothballed destroyers sails down the Hudson as real and as startling as the ship *San Dominick* encountered in Melville's "Benito Cereno") and "The Sea of Hesitation" (where the narrator is beset by texts cascading from his past, including quotations from Civil War history and phone calls from his ex-wife).

What makes the volume different, however, and what justifies the author's resurrection of these older stories (which otherwise may have remained noncanonical, or at the very least so repetitious of outdated, minor trends that reprinting them would be redundant) is the function of the brief, italicized interleavings. These passages, never bearing a title and taking their table-of-contents identification from the egalitarianism of their opening words, form a larger continuous text in which the titled stories are set as intertexts. As a context for stories that are often about lives being lived within texts (movies, commercials, advertisements, letters, telephone calls, references to books and history), the interleavings have the latitude to speak either more abstractly or more specifically about such circumstances, and by doing so yield a continuity of literary action that shows how the otherwise diverse weavings of *Overnight to Many Distant Cities* are in fact cut from the same broad cloth—a multiform cloth to be sure, produced as it has been by the master weaver of stories, Donald Barthelme.

The situation of a typical story, "Affection," is a good example of how Barthelme's method works. Preceding it is the two-and-one-half-page passage beginning *"Financially, the paper"*; the narrative voice in this particular interpolation is that of a writer whose newspaper is financially healthy but journalistically weak, its portfolio fattened by diversification into everything from mining to greeting cards and its real-estate, food, clothing, plant, and furniture sections growing larger each week, at the same time that hard news and editorial depth suffer. Typically for the times, the problem is being treated systematically, even as the system in question (management levels) falters:

> The Editor's Caucus has once again applied to middle management for relief, and has once again been promised it (but middle management has Glenfiddich on its breath, even at breakfast). Top management's polls say that sixty-five percent of the readers "want movies," and feasibility studies are being conducted. Top management acknowledges, over long lunches at good restaurants, that the readers are wrong to "want movies" but insists that morality cannot be legislated. The newsroom has been insulated (with products from the company's Echotex division) so that the people in the newsroom can no longer hear the sounds in the streets. (O, p. 24)

Brief as it is, the interleaved passage profits from Barthelme's ability to take a limited number of factors—the newspaper's other divisions, the decline of its traditional standards, the lavish life style of its top management and the alcohol-ridden anxiety of the middle managers—and let their interactive energy combine to generate a tight little narrative. But in the setting of *Overnight to Many Distant Cities*, it performs a structural function as well, enfolding (with "*I put a name in an envelope* . . . ," which follows) the more conventionally written and published story, "Affection."

"Affection" itself features a newspaper only in its final paragraph, where its print is something that informs the husband-narrator (threatening to estrange him from his wife) but which also can be washed away (thus saving the marriage). Along the way to this conclusion are just the influences that have fattened up certain sections of the paper while slimming down others, although for the couple's life as lived these influences are encountered firsthand. The wife's chief advisor is her mother, whose "counsel is broccoli, mostly, but who else was she going to talk to?" (O, p. 30). When the husband consults his own advisor, Madam Olympia, her patois rendering of a typical marital conversation uncovers the "agendas on both sides" (O, p. 31). Subsequent textual renderings come from the languages of TV soap opera, psychiatry, and the blues. As for the couple's problems, they're solved only by a sudden influx of new money—something wily Madam Olympia has expected would have to happen from the start.

From here Barthelme moves to an abstract piece, "*I put a name in an envelope* . . . ," which first appeared as part of *Joseph Cornell: Catalogue of the Exhibition, February 28–March 20, 1976*, published by the Leo Castelli Gallery. In the unpaged catalog's preface, designer-editor Sandra Leonard Starr thanks the author, "who has loved Cornell's work for a very long time, for saying he couldn't think of anything to write and writing anyway." Its apparent abstraction and self-advertised insouciance do not detract from its fictive excellence, both in itself and as an interpolation within *Overnight to Many Distant Cities*; in fact, the piece is as well organized and as indicative of Barthelme's aesthetic as his catalog preface to the exhibit of women in art from 2500 B.C. to the present, *She* (New York: Cordier & Ekstrom Gallery, 3 December 1970 to 16 January 1971). There the author had posited woman as an imaginary being, an absent referent present only in the empty space she would otherwise be occupying. For Joseph Cornell, Barthelme casts out a similar net, retrieves nothing, but discovers that Cornell has become his net. For the Castelli catalog, he presents a single page typed on his own IBM Selectric; photocopied in facsimile fashion, it is folded twice and placed in an envelope, just as its first line describes; the stuffed envelope then becomes one of the several loose items gathered into the catalog, which is itself a two-pocket folder holding several individual pages and photographs. Reading the catalog thus becomes much like viewing a Cornell artwork, as the various free-standing yet compositionally integral elements are sorted out and comprehended both as entities and as parts of a whole. Reading Barthelme's page in the catalog or on the pages in *Overnight to Many Distant Cities* replicates this process, and in the latter case also supplies a context for "Affection" preceding it and "Lightning" to follow.

Like one of Joseph Cornell's boxes, Barthelme's page recycles discrete but personally treasured items in a way that produces a new artistic whole. "Affection" has shown an unhappily married couple doing much the same with the fragmented texts of their lives, the bonding agent being another printed text: money. "Lightning" poses a single protagonist who must deal with similar intertexts even as he struggles to write and live one of his own. Freelancing for a *People*-like weekly called *Folks*, he must take assignments on human-interest topics (such as people struck by lightning); the story's length is dictated by concerns of layout, while its focus must be, in his editor's words, on a subject who is not only "pretty sensational" but "slightly wonderful" (O, p. 41). His own career as a writer has taken him down a path much like the husband's in "Affection," compromising ideals in order to earn more money to please his wife; but at this later stage he has lost his wife and quit the job for the textual bliss of freelancing according to his whims and fancies, with just the occasional high-paying job for *Folks* to keep him in rent and liquor.

This writer's human-interest feature on interesting people struck by lightning turns out to be a harvesting of recycled parts: nearly every one of his subjects has a grandparent who was struck by lightning as well (usually struck off a buckboard in 1910) and has fastened on an authoritative text to interpret his or her event. The writer himself becomes format-driven, blanching when a second respondent also has a husband named Marty—

"Two Martys in the same piece?" (O, p. 44). But at this point he is figuratively struck by lightning himself, falling in love with this woman who is not only slightly wonderful but capable of enfolding him within the text of her own life, made as it is of trendy, manufactured images. Drunk with love, he tries to seduce her with a story generated out of fragments from his public relations work for Texas oil. But all that succeeds is the Folks layout, expanded as it is for this woman of his dreams who has become, in his editor's words, "approximately fantastic" (O, p. 51).

Through these stories and their interleavings Barthelme has woven a larger text whose strands remain distinct even as they become mutually enhancing. As intertextual elements exist within the volume's full-length New Yorker stories, so do those stories themselves function intertextually within the collection's larger narrative movement as carried forth by the italicized interleavings. By themselves, Overnight's titled stories are reminiscent of an earlier Barthelme or, as with "Captain Blood," of Barthelme's colleagues in postmodern fiction—one thinks of Robert Coover's classic reversal of the Casey at the Bat narrative, "McDuff on the Mound," when reading Barthelme's hilarious account of a textually correct but contextually inappropriate John Paul Jones speaking his historic lines prematurely and to the wrong auditor. Arranged as they are in Overnight, however, these stories not only reinforce each other, as should happen in a decently arranged collection, but are situated within a larger whole that the interleavings sustain. Should the reader wonder what type of literature is "Captain Blood," there follows an interleaving in the form of conceptual art, "A woman seated on a plain wooden chair . . . ," the nature of which suggests that there can be conceptual fiction as well (which "Captain Blood" certainly is). If "Conversations with Goethe" seems at first like a single-joke story (the master's one-sided conversations consisting of aphoristic similes rushing pell-mell into absurdity), the interleaving that follows draws directly on American popular culture to show how the same thing happens when the fans of country and western music dote on the lyrics of their heroes. Finally, in the volume's title story, the larger narrative concludes with these italicized interpolations incorporated directly into the text.

Four years later, in the volume complementing Sixty Stories and rounding off his hundred presumably best stories, Donald Barthelme reprints

"Overnight to Many Distant Cities." But among these Forty Stories are no less than eleven others from the Overnight volume, more than from any single collection recalled for service in his first retrospective. True, Forty Stories also takes a second sampling from books as far back as Unspeakable Practices, Unnatural Acts, and draws so many additional pieces from City Life and especially Sadness as to make those collections' representation among the favored hundred almost complete, with only the extremes of obtuseness ("Bone Bubbles") and obviousness ("Brain Damage," "Perpetua," and "Subpoena") missing. Yet the special nature of Overnight to Many Distant Cities as an integral volume is lost, for the stories are not only presented in a different order (as Barthelme had done for the collections covered in Sixty Stories) but are scattered throughout Forty Stories almost randomly, a departure from his earlier retrospective practice of keeping each volume's selections together. As a final blow to Overnight's special nature, the typographical and titular distinctions between the mainline stories and the interpolations are effaced, making each one just one more equal addition to the Barthelme canon.

The special task of Forty Stories, however, is to complete an even larger whole—a whole much greater than the sum of its individual parts. In this sense, the material comprising Overnight to Many Distant Cities can be read two ways: as a volume that can stand alone almost as easily and completely as do any of the author's novels, or serving as examples of his short story artistry, twelve of which he selects, along with nine quite recent and therefore previously uncollected stories, to represent the latest developments in his work.

These twenty-one pieces reveal a Barthelme as comfortable and as playful as the writer Sixty Stories portrays, but also as an author committed to drawing openly and directly on his own experience. In stories such as "Visitors," "Affection," and "Lightning" (all of which are reprinted here), bits and pieces of Donald Barthelme's life could be recognized, but were always couched within the conventions of fiction: different names, similar but not identical professions, and only a generalized reference to locale (Texas, but not specifically Houston; New York City, but only occasionally an address identifiable as Greenwich Village). But by choosing his unsigned New Yorker "Comment" piece identified as "When he came . . ." in Overnight to *Many Distant Cities* and running it as a full-fledged, co-equal story under the title of "The New Owner," Barthelme takes a step as obvious as when selecting his parodies and satires (previously sequestered in *Guilty Pleasures*) for canonization in *Sixty Stories*. In 1978, for a limited edition titled *Here in the Village* published with the Lord John Press in Northridge, California, he had gathered up eleven such unsigned columns and added his Cordier & Ekstrom catalog preface on images of women in art to form an entertaining, engaging, and self-exploratory look at the real Donald Barthelme living on New York's West 11th Street. Even as that volume appeared, the text presented as "The New Owner" in *Forty Stories* was being debuted as an unsigned "Comment" essay in *The New Yorker* for December 4, 1978, leading off the magazine's editorial section on page 21. From here its progress is revealing, not just because it brings an element of *Here in the Village* into *Overnight to Many Distant Cities*, but because even that presence, interpolative as it was, now becomes mainstream in the retrospective collection that rounds out Barthelme's career as a short story writer.

Of the author's signed *New Yorker* stories published since *Overnight*, only "Kissing the President" (August 1, 1983) is passed over. Of the nine included, a few tend toward abstraction, but the great majority are evocative of experiences and locales in Barthelme's very real world. The 1980s had seen him return home to Texas for part of each year and a chair at the University of Houston, his alma mater, and in "Sinbad" he unites the abstract and referential streams of his later work by crafting a story in which the protagonist is at once Sinbad the Sailor washed up on the figurative beach of middle age at the same time he's teaching a writing class at an all too typical southwestern university, where he rescues a failing pedagogic situation by realizing "I have something to teach. Be like Sinbad! Venture forth! Embosom the waves, let your shoes be sucked from your feet and your very trousers enticed by the frothing deep. The ambiguous sea awaits, I told them, marry it!" (FS, p. 34).

"The point of my career is perhaps how little I achieved" (FS, p. 256), concludes the journalist-turned-religion-writer being interviewed in "January," *Forty Stories*' last selection. As a piece of fiction, it interrogates itself—how odd that for all of Donald Barthelme's experiments with form, he waits until almost the very end before trying the same format so many critics, including myself, had used to generate texts, presenting him with studious questions to which he would reply in kind, much as does the character Thomas Brecker in this piece. The point of "January," however, is that viewing a lifetime's remarkable achievements as "so little" is the best way to keep one's self alive. The title, after all, is not "November" or "December," but rather the year's coldest month, the depth of winter, which is nevertheless the start of something entirely new. Forty Stories, providing as it does the larger context and canonical status for Here in the Village, may well be the January of Barthelme's career—not as a living author but as one for the ages.

Epilogue:

The Text in the Village

H ere in the Village (1978) is the gathering of texts generated in the world where I met Donald Barthelme. First published (with one exception) as unsigned editorial comments in The New Yorker, they have no basis for being considered canonical, postmodern, or even critically important for Barthelme's career until the next decade, when similar pieces are used as untitled italicized interpolations to structure Overnight to Many Distant Cities and ultimately given titles and the uniformity of roman typeface for inclusion as mainline fictions in Forty Stories. One could argue, of course, that the presence of this world makes itself felt in such signed stories as "Bishop," "Visitors," and other fictions drawing on life in the West Village. But in terms of the author's incidental publications, which also include The Slightly Irregular Fire Engine (1971), Sam's Bar (1987), and his posthumously issued The King (1990), this collection of "Comment" pieces is best studied on its own terms, as a small press limited edition (just 325 copies) that catches Donald Barthelme at an interesting point in both his personal and professional life: newly (and finally stably) remarried, with the modernist dead father of his writing career finally buried and the whole new world of a liberated postmodernism open before him.

This world of Greenwich Village, the West Village in particular, is evident in Barthelme's writing, but equally important is Barthelme's presence in the neighborhood. He'd been fortunate to be at the same address since 1962, subletting to Tom Wolfe for a year when abroad on a Guggenheim Fellowship. A house-proud renter, Barthelme took obvious pleasure in his tenancy on West Eleventh Street, and felt a loss when, on his return from Denmark, he found that the fine tree shading his building's front yard had died. "Rumor had it," he told me, "that Tom did a lot of staring out the window." From this block between busy Seventh Avenue and trendy Sixth, Don could venture out into a world possessing the coherency of a domestic neighborhood and the excitement of one of the world's greatest cities. Editorial offices could be a world away, if he wished; in the Village he would hide out when he felt like it, knowing that across the street was Grace Paley and down the block a number of other close friends ready to give personal as well as professional sustenance.

This world and Don's role in it figure throughout *Here in the Village* and later in *Sam's Bar* (where the dash-dialogue method finds graphic form in Seymour Chwast's cartoons), but they also make a special guest appearance on the cover of Stephen Dixon's book of integrated short fictions, *Quite Contrary: The Mary and Newt Story* (New York: Harper & Row, 1979). In Mark Alan Stamaty's cartoon gracing this dust jacket Dixon appears in a third floor window, surveying a street corner scene that is unmistakably the intersection of Sixth Avenue and West Eleventh Street. In Stamaty's patented style, human pedestrians brush shoulders with animals such as a tweed-suited rhino and a friendly alligator coming out the door of a delicatessen. The Avenue is clogged with traffic, and for added clamor there's a car zooming up the side of a building. Interesting people are everywhere, one of the happiest and most involved being a tall, sharp-bearded man coming around the corner: Donald Barthelme.

Stamaty's juxtaposition of the strange and the familiar all mixed together in such a marvelous whirl of invention would have been an appropriate jacket cover for *Here in the Village*. In his preface to the volume Barthelme explains how his writing both draws from and relates to the community, *The New Yorker's* Notes and Comment section giving him the chance to "appear on Wednesday (when the magazine is generally available in New York) being mad about whatever one was overstimulated by on Tuesday of the previous week or whenever the piece was written" (*HV*, p. 9). In the first of the volume's dozen selections (none of which are titled), Barthelme does just this: in the Barthesean manner of experiencing (and then writing) as an intransitive act, the narrator simply walks around the Village and takes note of the multiform things happening to him. The closest bellestristic analogue would be another writer's work that was influenced even more directly by Roland Barthes, Peter Handke's *Das Gewicht der Welt* (Salzburg: Residenz Verlag, 1977), translated with Ralph Mannheim and revised by Handke as *The Weight of the World* (New York: Farrar, Straus & Giroux, 1984). Like Handke, he is identifiable as who he is, and reacts in character, in this case by walking over to the nearby site of the former Women's House of Detention, which is being developed into a pretty little park. For that, Barthelme is grateful, but even more so because of the memory this absent building holds:

> The Women's House of Detention was the place where they used to store women arrested for prostitution, mostly. The thing I remember about it best, aside from its social inutility and hideousness, is that one time a pal of mine who was in the anti-war-activist business got situated there because she had sat down in front of an Armed Forces Day parade. And it stopped, for a while. Anyhow, she was put in a cell with a woman who was in that other business, and that woman asked her what she was in for, and my pal told her. And the other woman immediately rushed to the cell door and yelled at the turnkey, *"Get these fucking housewives outta here!"* Anyhow, the planting is going in, and it looks mighty good. (HV, pp. 11–12)

In less than a paragraph, Barthelme visits both present and past, encountering not just something in the neighborhood but a memory of a favorite good neighbor, Grace Paley, whose imprisonment had reinforced his understanding of the building's "social inutility" and now does the same for the reader, who is gifted with a great line from the prostitute as a way of settling the same point. Unifying the vignette is its introductory news that "I don't know who is the genius" for getting this planting done, "but I take my hat off to her" (HV, p. 11).

This initial Comment column continues with other encounters: bumping into the wife of his building's superintendent at the corner liquor store, visiting a friend at St. Vincent's Hospital (which is also nearby), being threatened by a junior version of a street gang, and sharing a dance at a local street festival. From each occasion Barthelme takes home a good line and a telling memory, just as Peter Handke's habit of prowling his Parisian neighborhood and making note of things provides him with not only a

Cover illustration by Mark Alan Stamaty for
Quite Contrary by Stephen Dixon.

book's worth of material but over a year's worth of writerly sustenance—
in each case a way of being in the world and on the page at the same time.
Conventionally, there are little dramas to be observed. In *Das Gewicht der
Welt* a very old man finds the local grocery out of his preferred small-size
box of salt and reluctantly buys the larger package, remarking that the last
packet had lasted three years; Handke notes a strange silence in the shop,
as everyone suddenly realizes that the gentleman has just bought his last

container of salt. In this initial piece from Here in the Village, the author finds himself caught within his friends' dialogue over their suicidal daughter's hospital bed, "which was whether the attempt had been serious or not" (HV, p. 13). The wife thinks it has been; the husband thinks not. The author kicks the husband in the leg several times while patting him calmly until the man realizes he's just scared, has been babbling, and shuts up. But for the most part Barthelme's and Handke's encounters with the world are handled in a postmodern manner: nonhierarchical, nonjudgmental, playful rather than purposeful, oriented toward process rather than product, deconstructive rather than totalizing, and directed less toward a probe for deep meaning than toward a fascination with surface. In the end, for all their writerly stimulus these texts become readerly, for the traditional compulsion to find meaning has yielded to the author's performance on the page, which the reader is invited to re-create.

From this initial selection, Here in the Village turns to other fascinations Barthelme has identified in his preface, including "the Oz-like city as a whole" and even national politics, since the Village is "not a bad place from which to hurl great flaming buckets of Greek fire (rhetoric) at the Government" (HV, p. 9). But throughout these pieces the author maintains an explicitly textual way of being in the world, from appreciating the personalized messages the electric company adds to his bill—"YOU HAVE AN EXCELLENT PAYMENT RECORD WITH US. THANK YOU!" (HV, p. 17)— to mocking the odd styles of language he's noted in reports from the intelligence community, including the remarkable term nondiscernible (HV, p. 20). No matter what happens, from his location here in the Village Barthelme can react as a member of the community, and in some cases that group becomes a community of writers. Grace Paley, of course, is across the street. But John Barth, William H. Gass, and Kurt Vonnegut are also neighbors in the free-floating commune of literary festivals, convention panels, and PEN/ American Center meetings, and from their habits and abilities he is able to draw up a proposal for writer-endorsements as marketable as any star athlete's commercial promotions. The author of such gargantuan novels as Giles Goat-Boy and the in-progress LETTERS could credibly recommend not only a good typewriter but a first-class typewriter cover, for "the big book demands a clean machine" (HV, p. 22). Vonnegut's Breakfast of Champions makes him a natural for the cereal crowd. A sharp travel agent might even advertise "the Tom Pynchon Getaway Adventure" (HV, p. 23).

When it comes to worrying about big government and big business on their own terms (and in their own language), Barthelme the Villager goes to the same source as do his characters in "Edward and Pia" (UP, p. 99): "Madam Cherokee, my Reader and Spiritual Advisor, who maintains premises on Orchard Street devoted, as it were, to pulling the teeth of the future" (HV, p. 26). Madam Cherokee speaks a jive lingo and reflects the moral posture of a street-wise operator in the world of small tricks and petty hustles; but when she answers serious questions about the latest financial news, her language and manner seem not only appropriate but shrewdly informative. As for the questions Donald Barthelme himself is asked, they are best answered with jokes, as in the author's published reply to a dead-serious questionnaire from Writer's Digest probing the presumed affinity "between hard drinking and the writing life" (HV, p. 32). When he does venture a serious opinion, it is on the really tough topics: the question of women (HV, pp. 41–44) and the problem of postmodernism (HV, pp. 37–40). Each is, as the postmodern philosophers themselves say, an absent referent, something never really present which is talked about nevertheless as if it is. Caught within the dance of each, Barthelme does not even try to identify the dancer. Instead, he probes the nature of these questions themselves. "Art, touching mysteries, tends to darken rather than illuminate them," he concludes. By becoming subjects for art, women in specific and postmodern notions in general become "momentarily free" (HV, p. 44), which is the moment in which he, as a fictionist rather than a commentator, prefers to be engaged.

It is on the level of art that Here in the Village concludes. Just as in Peter Handke's Das Gewicht der Welt, the impulse is to explore outward only to return to the writer's inner life, now revitalized by contact with the world but still ultimately regenerated by the author's own act of noting. Barthelme's second to last piece finds him prowling the city with a friend he calls Sweet Georgia Brown. Her patter is much like Madam Cherokee's, just as her own source of information, Blind Lightnin' Lemon Howlin' Brown, serves as a font of wisdom akin to Sweet Papa Cream Puff in "Affection" (O, p. 33). He is "the Elder Statesman of Pulling Your Coat to What's What"

(HV, p. 46), and as her parent is in an eminent position for transcending the dead father issue so critical to postmodern sons. His analysis, like Madam Cherokee's in the earlier selection, is quite telling: everything of value to the municipality and its citizens has been sold off, including the clichés of its language. Therefore it is time for the author to cast about for new bits of dialogue and useful one-liners.

Which is just what happens in the book's concluding selection. Beginning with an exclamation, "Spring in the Village!" (HV, p. 49), it serves as an upbeat complement to the walk around his neighborhood that begins the volume. There, the organizing principle was the nonhierarchal connectives that made it possible for the author to encounter and note the occasions for all those wonderful lines. Here, the circumstances are even more literary, as Barthelme cruises down the block to note the volumes stacked in neighbor Ramsey Clark's bay-window bookcases (all hardcovers) and the local grade school's entries in the contest organized by a restaurant expanding into larger quarters on the corner of Sixth Avenue and West Eleventh Street (all are extrapolations on the theme of "Ray's Pizza Is Getting Bigger"). Another eatery, Igor's Art Foods, features a Book of the Month display. "We are a bookish community," he concludes (HV, p. 50).

"We are a community of writers" as well, for in the next line Barthelme bumps into Norman Mailer. "What does it feel like to know that your [next] novel must be worth a million dollars, more or less, before you write it? He is a brave man" (HV, p. 50). Barthelme will never be a writer of this financial magnitude; nor will the bag lady scrawling something on the wall as he and Mailer pass. But they are, all three, a community, which is the paragraph's apt concluding line.

Students from P. S. 41 illustrate a text, while the bag lady comments on another—such is the world Donald Barthelme inhabits, even as neighborhood committees organize to protest library cuts and laundromat bulletin boards, "the jungle drums of the Village" (HV, p. 52), are filled with announcements for readings and for the recovery of a commemorative plaque stolen from the nearby building that housed D. W. Griffith's early studio. There is even an invitation for another text: "Runaway wife sought by female reporter for indepth interview" (HV, p. 52). The most telling message, however, is the one our author reads in the person of a new visitor:

> Meandering down Hudson Street, thinking about lunch, I see in the back seat of a Dodge with Tennessee plates a sleeper who has wrapped himself in Reynolds Wrap to ward off the fine midmorning Village light. I am happy and know myself to be happy—a rare state. Good luck to you, traveller from Tennessee! (HV, p. 52)

In 1962, Donald Barthelme had himself arrived from Texas and wrapped himself in just such reflective trappings, as a witty and urbane commentator on the world of art. From West Eleventh Street he found his way from *Location* to *The New Yorker* without having to give up the sense of community he had so fortunately discovered in the West Village. Now, with *Here in the Village*, he embraces the full geography of his textual world—even the art criticism he would continue pursuing to the end of his life. From this position he is able to convey blessings to all, just as his world blesses him with daily gifts of language and circumstance.

From here it is a short step to Barthelme's Notes and Comment writings' taking their place in his fictive canon. Hints of it had appeared as early as June 13, 1970, when his first recorded contribution appeared: untitled and unsigned like all such *New Yorker* front matter to follow, but eventually incorporated into "Flying to America" and again into "A Film" (*Sadness*) and "Two Hours to Curtain" (*Guilty Pleasures*). Evidence for the method's eventual canonization comes with "The Teachings of Don B.: A Yankee Way of Knowledge," first published in the *New York Times Magazine* for February 11, 1973 (pp. 14–15, 66–67) and gathered with similar satires and parodies in *Guilty Pleasures*. But the most conclusive moves come in the wake of *Here in the Village*, where structurally, tonally, and topically identical pieces are published as mainline short stories in *The New Yorker* and promoted from interpolative status in *Overnight to Many Distant Cities* to full-fledged fictions in *Forty Stories*. In "Sakrete" we see a story from *The New Yorker* of October 10, 1983, appear six weeks later as "On our street . . ." in *Overnight* (pp. 145–49) and then reassume its initial role in *Forty Stories* (pp. 193–96), even as its essence remains indistinguishable from *Overnight*'s "When he came . . ." (pp. 107–9), a Comment piece from December 4, 1978, not given a title ("The

New Owner") until the final omnibus volume (FS, pp. 77–79). All along this way, readers see the same narrative figure living at the same address and reacting to a by-now familiar world. Who is this man? The most scientifically correct description comes in the parody of Carlos Castenada's *The Teachings of Don Juan: A Yaqui Way of Knowledge* that opens the "Teachings of Don B." piece:

> While doing anthropological field work in Manhattan some years ago I met, on West Eleventh Street, a male Yankee of indeterminate age whose name, I was told, was Don B. I found him leaning against a building in a profound torpor—perhaps the profoundest torpor I have ever seen. He was a tallish man with an unconvincing beard and was dressed, in the fashion of the Village, in jeans and a blue work shirt. . . . I expressed a wish to learn what he knew and asked if I might talk with him about the subject. He simply stared at me without replying and then said, "No." However, taking note of the dismay which must have been plain on my face, he said that I might return, if I wished, in two years. In the meantime, he would think about my proposal. Then he closed his eyes again, and I left him.
>
> I returned in the summer of 1968 and found Don B. still leaning against the same building. . . . He then led me into the building against which he had been leaning. He showed me into a small but poorly furnished apartment containing hundreds of books stacked randomly about. In the center of the room a fire was blazing brightly. Throwing a few more books on the fire, Don B. invited me to be seated, and we had the first of what proved to be a long series of conversations. The following material, produced from my field notes. . . . (GP, pp. 53–54)

From the field notes of my own conversations with Don B. and from my researches among the textual artifacts of his literary being have come the materials to get this study under way. Some clues have been bibliographical, such as finding hints of his writing method in the progression from unsigned Comment pieces to various formats in his subsequent collections. Lines Don gave me for interviews—in person, by letter, and over the phone—would show up, sometimes a decade later, in his short stories. Even more interesting was how certain interpretations, such as collage being the dominant principle of modern art (broached in a 1971 letter and eventually published in 1974 when our interview appeared in editor Joe David Bellamy's *The New Fiction*), would develop over the years into much more sophisticated (and postmodernist) theories, notably his suggestion in the exhibition catalog for *Robert Rauschenberg: Work from the Four Series* (Houston: Contemporary Arts Museum, 1985) that silkscreen might be an even better metaphor for how his and other postmodern writing stood in relation to referential subjects.

"Being Bad" is his title for this little piece, one of his last but happiest on the art world that had drawn him to New York and provided both inspiration and affinity. He describes a visit in 1962 to Rauschenberg's studio, where he could delight in the visual image, ready-made for a photo page in *Location*, of the loft's grimy windows catching the tone of the artist's current black-and-white silkscreen paintings. In these works, Barthelme notes, was a transfiguration of the commonplace that transcended "mere run-of-the-mill outrageousness" and became instead something central to the transformational process "by which aspects of the world are made over into art." Yet even this early in Rauschenberg's career Barthelme fears a loss of impact, a softening of this proclaimed messiness into something conventionally beautiful. Therefore it is with relief and satisfaction that in 1985 he can review Rauschenberg's *oeuvre* and marvel that "to sustain a high level of misbehavior over a third of a century is not the easiest of tasks." The key is not just the artist's (or the writer's) quotation, as has always been possible in collage, but how the quotation may now be made:

> The photomechanical silkscreen, too, expands the bin of materials available to the collagist enormously. It provides access to anything that has ever been photographed, allows quotation at great length and at any scale. It permits superimposition of one image upon another in such a way that the first bleeds through the second, as physical collage does not—that is, it allows a heightened degree of messiness. (RR, p. 8)

There must be a construction, Barthelme concludes, that holds the viewer in a particular type of tension, "and it is in being able to pull this off, year after year, that major reputations are made and endure." If the principle of collage is "the juxtapositions of unlike things within a visual field," then silkscreen is such juxtaposition without having to ignore the "true source" of the artist's power, "which lies in the mystery of particular choices" (RR, p. 9).

It is a common fact, Barthelme the storyteller often hints, that when we pretend to be speaking about angels, we are really speaking about men and women existing quite naturally among us. Knowing his ideals and demands for his own literary art, it is not unlikely that in these words about Robert Rauschenberg's work he is actually referring to his own.

Bibliography

Abbreviations are indicated when a work cited in the text has not been identified by its full title. An asterisk indicates that no abbreviation was used.

I. Fiction by Donald Barthelme

CB *Come Back, Dr. Caligari*. Boston: Little, Brown & Co., 1964.

SW *Snow White*. New York: Athenaeum, 1967.

UP *Unspeakable Practices, Unnatural Acts*. New York: Farrar, Straus & Giroux, 1968.

CL *City Life*. New York: Farrar, Straus & Giroux, 1970.

*   *The Slightly Irregular Fire Engine*. New York: Farrar, Straus & Giroux, 1971.

S   *Sadness*. New York: Farrar, Straus & Giroux, 1972.

GP *Guilty Pleasures*. New York: Farrar, Straus & Giroux, 1974.

DF *The Dead Father*. New York: Farrar, Straus & Giroux, 1975.

A   *Amateurs*. New York: Farrar, Straus & Giroux, 1976.

GD *Great Days*. New York: Farrar, Straus & Giroux, 1979.

*   *The Emerald*. Los Angeles: Sylvester and Orphanos, 1980 [reprinted without collages in SS].

*   *Presents*. Dallas: Pressworks, 1980 [reprinted from *Penthouse* 9, no. 4 (December 1977): 106–10, with new collages pasted in].

SS *Sixty Stories*. New York: Putnam's, 1981.

O   *Overnight to Many Distant Cities*. New York: Putnam's, 1983.

P   *Paradise*. New York: Putnam's, 1986.

*   *Sam's Bar* (with Seymour Chwast). New York: Doubleday, 1987.

*   *The King*. New York: Harper & Row, 1990.

II. Selected Nonfiction by Donald Barthelme

*   "The Emerging Figure." Contemporary Arts Museum [Houston] Catalog, May–June, 1961. Text reprinted in Forum [University of Houston] 3, no. 2 (Summer 1961): 23–24.

*   "After Joyce." *Location* 1, no. 2 (Summer 1964): 13–16.

*   Untitled preface to *she*. Catalog for an exhibition at the Cordier & Ekstrom Gallery, New York, 3 December 1970 to 16 January 1971 [reprinted in *HV* with the introductory phrase, "Worrying about women"].

*   Untitled commentary on his story "Paraguay." *Writer's Choice*, edited by Rust Hills. New York: David McKay, 1974, pp. 25–26.

*   Untitled preface to *Robert Morris*. Catalog for an exhibition at the Washburn Gallery, New York, 10 February to 6 March 1970.

*   "Cornell." Contribution to the portfolio-catalog designed by Sandra Leonard Starr for the Joseph Cornell exhibition at the Leo Castelli Gallery, New York, 28 February–20 March 1976 [reprinted in *Ontario Review*, 5 (Fall-Winter 1976–1977): 50, and as "I put a name in an envelope . . ." in *O*].

HV   *Here in the Village*. Northridge, Calif.: Lord John Press, 1978.

*   "As Grace Paley Faces Jail with 3 Other Writers." *New York Times* [Op-Ed page], 2 February 1979, p. A25.

*   "Not Knowing." In *Voicelust*, edited by Allen Weir and Don Hendrie, Jr. Lincoln: University of Nebraska Press, 1985, pp. 37–50.

RR   "Being Bad." Preface to *Robert Rauschenberg: Work from the Four Series, a Sesquicentennial Exhibition*, Houston: Contemporary Arts Museum, 1985, pp. 8–9.

III. Selected Interviews and Symposia with Donald Barthelme

Brans, Jo. "Embracing the World: An Interview with Donald Barthelme." *Southwest Review* 67 (Spring 1982): 121–37.

Klinkowitz, Jerome. "Donald Barthelme." In *The New Fiction*, edited by Joe David Bellamy. Urbana: University of Illinois Press, 1974, pp. 45–54.

McCaffery, Larry. "An Interview with Donald Barthelme." In *Anything Can Happen: Interviews with Contemporary American Novelists*, edited by Tom LeClair and Larry McCaffery. Urbana: University of Illinois Press, 1983, pp. 32–44.

Wood, Susan. "High Priest of Trash and Flesh." *Houston City Magazine* 3, no. 3 (February 1979): 31–34, 36.

Unsigned. "A Symposium on Fiction" [Donald Barthelme, Grace Paley, Walker Percy, and William H. Gass]. *Shenandoah* 27 (Winter 1976): 3–31.

IV. Critical Sources

Barth, John. *The Friday Book*. New York: Putnam's, 1984.

Barthes, Roland. *The Eiffel Tower and Other Mythologies*. New York: Hill & Wang, 1979. Translated by Richard Howard from *Mythologies* (Paris: Seuil, 1957) and *La Tour Eiffel* (Paris: Delpire, 1964).

———. *The Fashion System*. New York: Hill & Wang, 1983. Translated by Matthew Ward and Richard Howard from *Système de la Mode* (Paris: Seuil, 1967).

———. *Mythologies*. New York: Hill & Wang, 1972. Translated by Annette Lavers from *Mythologies* (Paris: Seuil, 1957).

———. *Roland Barthes*. New York: Hill & Wang, 1977. Translated by Richard Howard from *Roland Barthes par Roland Barthes* (Paris: Seuil, 1975).

———. *S/Z: An Essay*. New York: Hill & Wang, 1974. Translated by Richard Miller from *S/Z* (Paris: Seuil, 1970).

Beckett, Samuel. "Dante . . . Bruno. Vico . . . Joyce." In *I Can't Go On, I'll Go On*, edited by Richard W. Seaver. New York: Grove Press, 1976, pp. 107–26.

Bruss, Paul. *Victims: Textual Strategies in Recent American Fiction*. Lewisburg, Penn.: Bucknell University Press, 1981.

Couturier, Maurice, and Régis Durand. *Donald Barthelme*. London: Methuen, 1982.

Dixon, Stephen. *Quite Contrary: The Mary and Newt Story*. New York: Harper & Row, 1979.

Foucault, Michel. *The Archaeology of Knowledge*. New York: Pantheon, 1972. Translated by Alan Sheridan from *L'archéologie du savior* (Paris: Gallimard, 1969).

Gardner, John. *On Moral Fiction*. New York: Basic Books, 1978.

Gordon, Lois. *Donald Barthelme*. Boston: Twayne Publishers, 1981.

Graff, Gerald. *Literature against Itself*. Chicago: University of Chicago Press, 1979.

Handke, Peter. *The Weight of the World*. New York: Farrar, Straus & Giroux, 1984. Translated with Ralph Mannheim from *Das Gewicht der Welt* (Salzburg: Residenz Verlag, 1977).

Hassan, Ihab. *The Dismemberment of Orpheus: Toward a Postmodern Literature*. 2nd ed. Madison: University of Wisconsin Press, 1982.

———. *The Literature of Silence*. New York: Knopf, 1967.

———. *The Postmodern Turn*. Columbus: Ohio State University Press, 1987.

Hendin, Josephine. *Vulnerable People: A View of American Fiction since 1945*. New York: Oxford University Press, 1978.

Karl, Frederick R. *American Fictions 1940–1980*. New York: Harper & Row, 1983.

Klinkowitz, Jerome. *The Life of Fiction*. Urbana: University of Illinois Press, 1977.

———. *Literary Disruptions: The Making of a Postcontemporary American Fiction*. 2nd ed. Urbana: University of Illinois Press, 1980.

McCaffery, Larry. *The Metafictional Muse: The Works of Robert Coover, Donald Barthelme, and William H. Gass*. Pittsburgh: University of Pittsburgh Press, 1982.

Molesworth, Charles. *Donald Barthelme's Fiction: The Ironist Saved from Drowning*. Columbia: University of Missouri Press, 1982.

Rosenberg, Harold. *The Tradition of the New*. New York: Horizon Press, 1959.

Roth, Philip. *Reading Myself and Others*. New York: Farrar, Straus & Giroux, 1975.

Schickel, Richard. *The Disney Version*. New York: Simon & Schuster, 1968.

Stengel, Wayne B. *The Shape of Art in the Short Stories of Donald Barthelme*. Baton Rouge: Louisiana State University Press, 1985.

Sukenick, Ronald. *In Form: Digressions on the Act of Fiction*. Carbondale: Southern Illinois University Press, 1985.

Wilde, Alan. *Horizons of Assent: Modernism, Postmodernism, and the Ironic Imagination*. Baltimore: Johns Hopkins University Press, 1981.

———. *Middle Grounds: Studies in Contemporary American Fiction*. Philadelphia: University of Pennsylvania Press, 1987.

V. Bibliographies

Klinkowitz, Jerome, Asa B. Pieratt, Jr., and Robert Murray Davis. *Donald Barthelme: A Comprehensive Bibliography*. Hamden, Conn.: Shoestring Press / Archon Books, 1977.

Klinkowitz, Jerome. "Donald Barthelme." *Literary Disruptions*. 2nd ed. Urbana: University of Illinois Press, 1980, pp. 252–62.

Index

About the Author

Jerome Klinkowitz is a professor of English and
University Distinguished Scholar at the University of
Northern Iowa. He is the author of twenty-five
books, including *Literary Disruptions: The Making of a Post-
Contemporary American Fiction*, *Kurt Vonnegut*, and *Short
Season and Other Stories*.

_____

Library of Congress Cataloging-in-Publication Data
Klinkowitz, Jerome.
Donald Barthelme : an exhibition / Jerome
Klinkowitz.
Includes bibliographical references and index.
ISBN 0-8223-1152-6
1. Barthelme, Donald—Criticism and interpretation.
2. Postmodernism (literature)—United States.
I. Title.
PS3552.A76Z75   1991
813'.54—dc20   90-27833   CIP